The
Secrets
of Investing
in Technology
Stocks

The
Secrets
of Investing
in Technology
Stocks

EDWARD TRAPUNSKI

JOHN WILEY & SONS
Toronto • New York • Chichester • Weinheim • Brisbane • Singapore

John Wiley & Sons Canada Limited
22 Worcester Road, Etobicoke, Ontario, M9W1L1

Canadian Cataloguing in Publication Data

Trapunski, Edward, 1947-
   The secrets of investing in technology stocks

Includes index.
ISBN 0-471-64236-3

1. Stocks.   2. High technology industries.   I. Title.

HG4661.T73 1998   332.63'22   C98-930066-8

Production Credits
Cover: Christine Kurys, RGD
Text design: JAQ, RGD
Printer: Tri-Graphic Printing

Printed in Canada
10 9 8 7 6 5 4 3 2 1

CONTENTS

PREFACE

What Makes Investing in Technology Stocks Special?

In certain circles, I have a particular allure as a man of mystery. I write about technology as well as financial services and institutions. Both are areas that both fascinate and perplex people. Those who travel the technology trails regard investing and finance as something mysterious and arcane. "I know so much about technology. If only I knew how to capitalize on this knowledge to make myself some money," my propeller-head buddies lament. They hear about the latest and the greatest technological advances, but they don't know how to follow through and turn a profit.

Those in the financial world view technology as cryptic and abstruse. I work in an office situated in the financial district and every day I rub shoulders with investors, brokers, money managers, and others whose lives revolve around securities. Since I am involved in various small capital ventures of my own, I come across business people who would like to score big in the sector of the stock market that is growing faster and returning greater profits than any other. If only they knew how. In this corporate circle, whenever I mention the latest technological development, the inevitable first question is "What should I invest in to make use of this information?"

With this book, I am bringing you wisdom from both worlds: the world of finance and the world of technology. Putting the two solitudes together can cut the risk and heighten the profits. Technology differs from any other investment. It follows its own code and subtleties. Even though it defies the rules, the first step is to understand the common-sense general principles of astute investment. Then comes the more discerning practice of applying them to the particular nuances of the technology business.

The Bigger the Risk, the Better the Reward

The rewards you can garner from this sector are greater than you can realize from any other. Throughout the good times and the bad, in a bull or a bear market, technology stocks have decisively outperformed the rest of the stock market. In the strong markets of the 1980s and 1990s, the technology sector has typically doubled the performance of the Dow Jones Industrial Average. But it follows, as any investor in any sector knows, that the greater the potential returns in an investment, the higher the risk..

Technology stocks bump up and down in price at their own rhythm. Generally, the rate at which these stocks move is much faster than the rest of the market. It is true that the technology business is influenced by the prevailing economy. After all, when times are tough, businesses are not inclined to equip their offices with the latest computers, and consumers are hesitant about even the snazziest cell phones. But more often than not, when you read a newspaper's daily analysis of the market, the headline refers to the effect of the technology sector on today's trading. Technology's influence on the stock market is pervasive.

The subsectors, or segments, that make up the technology group seem to have their own inscrutable impetus, flying high individualistically or crashing down to earth in unison. The so-called New Digital Industries, the segments that make up technology, include:

- electronic components like semiconductors and microchips;

- hardware and computers;

- computer peripherals comprising printers, modems and CD-ROMs;

- software that run businesses;

- telecommunications — the Internet;

- the wireless world;

- multimedia and graphics;

- entertainment and media, video games — consumer electronics;

- biotechnology and aerospace. (Because of the way they react, we are including these as part of the technology sector, though not everybody agrees they belong here.)

We will be discussing these segments in more detail in Part 2 of this book.

Are You Really Sure You Want to Do This?

This book doesn't come with a guarantee. Technology stocks are more volatile than virtually any other securities for sale on the stock market, and some people just don't have the stomach for it. It can keep you up nights and increase your intake of bicarbonate of soda. You know your own tolerance for risk, and you have to proceed at your own peril.

Investing in technology in the nineties is like buying into oil wells in the seventies. With a reference back to Mark Twain's famous aphorism that "a gold mine is a big hole in the ground with a liar on top," the joke in the seventies went that an oil well consisted of a hole in the ground and a promoter at the surface with a good story to tell, and in the nineties, you don't even need the hole, just the promoter with the story. With a technology company, if you strike the mother lode, it is better than black gold. But you have to be sure you are not drilling in a dry hole.

This book also doesn't come with the warning "Don't try this at home." In the stock market, as in life in general, you seldom regret what you have done, but you often regret what you could have done. Ten years from now, or five years, or six months, you don't want to hear yourself saying, "If I had only had Microsoft, or Intel, or Cisco," or whatever hot new technology you missed. For many investors, the exhilaration of hitting the big one outweighs any worries about risk.

If you had bought 1000 shares of Microsoft when it began trading in March 1986 at $2.33 (US), it would be worth $135,000 today and still moving up. The longest established specialized technology mutual fund, Baltimore-based T. Rowe Price Science and Technology Fund, has appreciated 300 times the average of all mutual funds. The only other specialized mutual fund sector that compares in growth is financial services.

The Psychology of the Technology Investor

Despite the inherent risk and volatility of the sector, everybody should consider investing in technology stocks. So much technology is being incorporated into our lives every day that even the most risk-averse investor is well served to have some degree

of exposure to it. If you want returns that are consistently exceptional, the technology sector is the place to find them. When
you look at what defines growth in today's economy, it's technology. The application of silicon and communications technology has a very big part to play in every portfolio. You cannot *not*
have technology in a well-balanced and diversified portfolio.

Having said that, it must be stated that success in this very
special sector requires a certain kind of psychology. It is not for
the fearful. Anybody who would be skittish or inclined to sell the
first time the stock price drops should probably think twice
about investing in technology stocks. But this sector has the
greatest growth stocks in the world, and if you want a major-
league home run — a four bagger — this is the sector for you.

Depending on factors such as age and personal goals, the
level of risk people are prepared to assume when building their
portfolio will differ. If you are in your twenties or early thirties
when volatility may not be so much of an concern, you are more
likely looking to buy the stocks that will give you the highest rate
of return rather than long-term stability. On the flip side, if you
are in your late forties or fifties, you will probably want to play
the market with much more caution.

A technology play takes patience. Sometimes you have to
wait it out to get the return you would like. Somebody who is
really going to need the money in the next two or three years to
buy a house or a car is probably better-off in a sector that is more
liquid. But for younger people who have disposable dollars to
risk it is well worthwhile. One doesn't do well every single time,
but if you are resilient enough to bounce back and try another
one, eventually you'll make money.

You can't make up for missed opportunities of the past, but
other opportunities are there for the future. However, it takes
fortitude, patience, and a special vision to find them.

The System

I am not a stockbroker, a cheerleader, or a soothsayer. I am a business journalist with no vested interest in convincing you about the wisdom of plunking your money down in this specific direction. I don't have any personal pet theories or systems that I want to sell you.

I'm not going to suggest specific securities because technology stock prices move so quickly. By the time you read this, today's hot technology might be yesterday's history. My goal is to help you make your own sharp decisions in this lucrative area by introducing you to the technology investment wizards and their ideas. I have benefited personally from following this market, and this book gives me the opportunity to draw on the perceptions of the best minds around. I have distilled their opinions and views, and I am sharing those perceptions with you here. In the pages of this book, you'll meet professional investors — analysts, personal money managers, and institutional and fund managers. You'll meet the technology company insiders with candid views about why some approaches work better than others. You'll meet individual investors with unbridled enthusiasm, some of whom are too bashful to trumpet their uncommon good luck and success. None of the people quoted here, even those with concealed or secret names, are composites. They are all real people. I am not too shy to let you know what my opinions are, but in the end, you will have the valuable tools to draw your own conclusions. If you win, thank me. If you lose, don't blame me.

I am also going to share the proceedings of the Victoria Investment Club of which I am a member. This club is made up of prominent computer scientists, analysts, consultants, marketers, and journalists, each with a specific knowledge about technology. The club meets biweekly to pool members' knowledge and discuss and invest in technology stocks. You will get an inside peek at the club's deliberations.

Understanding how the market works is vital in any sector, but it is especially so in this one. You can't choose technology stocks just with the standard investing principles of ratio, volume, or pattern. Instead this book will furnish the tips, techniques and strategies to help each investor judge a technology-related opportunity. It will help you to be able to choose wisely and make a fortune.

ACKNOWLEDGEMENTS

This book is about risk and reward. Many kind people took the risk of cooperating with me on this book and I hope my gratitude, and the benefits of helping investors, is enough of a reward. Leigh Whiting took the first risk by introducing me to Beth Bruder and Karen Milner of John Wiley & Sons Canada, Ltd., who, after one sushi lunch, heightened the risk by agreeing to publish *The Secrets of Investing in Technology Stocks*. Karen Milner, Ron Edwards, and Elizabeth McCurdy risked their patience by meticulously going over draft after draft of the manuscript. So many of the foremost practitioners in the financial and the technology industries took the risk of sharing their knowledge with me. Some of them are mentioned in the book, but many more aren't. I hope the reward for them is that their wisdom was properly interpreted. In doing research for the book, Aisha Wickham and her brother Olembe risked the exasperation of countless unfathomable requests for arcane information. My friends David Pyette and Alexandra Eadie risked the pestering for "just one more detail that needs verification." As peer reviewers, David Pyette, Haris Majeed, and Loudon Owen risked embarrassing me when they had to tell me when I didn't quite get it right. Paterson Mac-Dougall, Barristers and Solicitors, took the risk of inviting me to be author-in-residence while I completed the manuscript. Everybody at the law firm was kindly accepting of having a writer in their midst, but a special appreciation to Bruce MacDougall, Carol McCall, Peter Jacobsen, and my counsellor, Bruce Chambers, who were the first to decide that the risk of letting a writer loose among the lawyers wasn't extraordinary at all. The biggest risk, as usual, was taken by my wife Ellen Roseman, who let her husband pursue yet another risky project, and by my sons Richard and Charles, who accepted the risk of not having their father around very much. I missed them. I also want to acknowledge the lifelong risks of their late grandfathers, Abraham Trapunski and David Roseman, who both just missed the reward of seeing this book published.

Part 1

The Mystery of the Market

REVEALING THE CODE

The Peter Lynch Technology Technique

Peter Lynch, former manager of the Fidelity Magellan Fund and author of *One Up On Wall Street*, identified Dunkin' Donuts as one of his favourite investments. He said he never has to worry about someone inventing a better doughnut. It's a simple business and only location and freshness matter. Whereas when you buy a high-tech company, you don't know what the shelf-life of the product will be. And what are the chances that someone will come up with an innovation that's a little bit better or a little bit cheaper?

Investing in technology is generally not for the faint of heart. The speed with which the value of these stocks can change could give vertigo to even the most seasoned roller-coaster thrill-seeker. While the volatility tends to be high and the risks absolutely higher than in other sectors, the returns, when they come, can be worth the butterflies.

Technology is a growth area, not a cyclical one like automobiles or construction. It's not interest-rate sensitive like banks or utilities. It's not defensive like food or drugs, which are steadier than the average stock and relatively resistant to general economic changes. It's a sector that's not capital intensive. It's a sector that's very highly future oriented. And it's a sector that affects everybody.

Growth stocks have a natural upward bias. A decade ago, they constituted one-tenth of the North American economy. That figure is now about 20 per cent and by the year 2000 or 2001, economists confidently expect that growth industries will account for 25 per cent of the economy. Technology makes up about 12 per cent of the economy in the United States and 11 per cent in Canada.

There is no question we are shifting to a knowledge-based information technology economy. More and more issues of new companies fall into the technology sector, and it will not be long before they dominate the stock market. Almost 16 per cent of the Standard & Poor's 500 Composite index of stocks are technology stocks so that one could say the S&P is evolving into a science and technology stock index.

Despite this rapid evolution, most analysts say the high-tech sector is just entering an era of long-term growth. They are convinced that corporate spending on computers, communications, and related equipment will rise dramatically over the next few years. New ideas and concepts — basically high technology — is what drives the world.

Robert Ferchat is the chairman of the board and chief executive officer of BCE Mobile Communications Inc. and former president of its sister company, Northern Telecom Ltd. (Nortel). Mr. Ferchat is also successful at playing the stock market. Although he doesn't invest exclusively in technology stocks, he is partial to them and enjoys the good return he gets.

Investing in technology stocks has to do with your ability to discern new growth patterns, or new lifestyle patterns. As an investor, you get rewarded for judging whether or not a product or service has a broad market appeal, or is just a flash-in-the-pan technology that's interesting but that nobody is going to buy.

Robert Ferchat, CEO, BCE Mobile Communications Inc.

Finding out what these companies are worth is a formidable challenge for analysts. In other industries, value is affected by the ups and downs of the economic cycle or created by financial re-engineering such as cost-cutting or downsizing. Growth industries, most notably technology, are based on an idea that is waiting to be turned into a product or a service, and efficiency control doesn't seem to affect the bottom line in this sector. If the demand is there, it's there through good times and bad. Distribution, and meeting demand while the concept is hot, tend to be more important keys to hot returns.

It is precisely this unpredictability that makes this sector so attractive to some investors. Since patterns are hard to determine, technology investors like to boast that it takes more creativity, insight, and intellectual capacity to win in this sector. You can gloat about your success when the rest of the market is dejected. All of us have a contrarian streak in us that investing in this sector satisfies.

You may want to invest in technology stocks because you truly believe in the sector; or you may be looking for the one roll of the dice to hit the jackpot; or it could be one of the sectors you want to hold as a key part of a diversified portfolio; or you might dread heading to the millennium without a piece of the future in your pocket. Whatever the reasons, and all of these are valid, technology stocks are meant for the growth part of your portfolio. Investors don't buy them because they promise a gradual comfortable income like blue chips. They buy them because they can offer instant gratification by zooming up in value.

The timing for technology investing could not be better. It all began when, mainly spurred by the concept of creating semiconductor chips from silicon, the second most abundant element of the earth's crust, the science of computing boomed with invention overtaking invention. At the same time, the baby-boom generation woke up to the inevitability of retirement and began channelling its money into mutual funds. In an incredible coincidence of the right time and the right place, the baby-boomer money fuelled this environment of entrepreneurship and innovation. Investors, whose money deposited in funds and plans sparked an industry, are now affluent enough, and sophisticated enough, to invest their money directly in stocks.

The Roller-Coaster Market

Buy High, Sell Higher

The perennial investing question is how do you beat the market. The snide answer is: "Buy low and sell high." In the technology sector the realistic answer is: "Buy high, sell higher."

From the Experienced Investor

Since it is so marked by volatility and growth, it is difficult to present an accurate snapshot of the technology sector at any given moment. At the end of November 1997, notwithstanding a correction, the Canadian high-tech sector had gained over 30 per cent from the previous year. This despite a stock market that was tainted by the Bre-X scandal. At the same time in the United States, high-tech stocks surged to new highs, pulling the rest of the North American equity market up with them. There is no question that technology will continue to drive market performance. In one of the strongest bull markets ever recorded, technology stocks outstripped all others, rising, on average, more than three times as fast as the Toronto Stock Exchange 300 Index while the S&P hardware and software index performed almost twice as well as the less specialized, but large-cap-biased, S&P 500.

It is hard to identify a pattern in the technology sector because each segment, indeed each stock, seems to follow its own independent rhythm. Generally, the upward cycle begins in the fall, coinciding with new product initiatives and information flowing from the major trade shows like Comdex, and ends in the summer with a gentle sell-off.

Any number of factors can contribute to the movement of a technology stock, but none more dramatically than earnings momentum, either upward or downward. Technology stocks trade at multiples — price to earnings ratios — far exceeding the rest of the market, with investors basing their expectations more on potential earnings than on current earnings. However, these stocks always have to maintain the promise of future earnings. Investors watch the quarterly reports intently, and short-term earning results that don't meet projections can attack the value of a stock quickly and drastically.

In the stock market, especially the technology market, investor sentiment sways the direction of the price drastically. Investors are always checking to see what other people think, and basing their buy and sell decisions on "what the Street says." According to the "cockroach theory" of the stock market, if you see one, you can be sure there are many more around. In other words, when one analyst changes his or her opinion about the potential of a stock, you can be sure there are others lurking with reports that match the first one, which will trigger the momentum either up or down. Other factors such as new products and industry trends also have more of an impact than economic or seasonal cycles.

Technology Is Everywhere

From its beginnings, the stock market has been about technology. Among the first stocks traded on the London and New York stock exchanges were railroad shares, which was the new technology at the time. The railroad companies needed a huge influx of capital to finance the development of this technology. Later came the technology-driven automobile, electricity, telephone, and airplane companies, which came to the market with their newfangled ideas looking for investors.

At the end of the twentieth century, there are thousands of new technologies being created all the time. In 1997, there were 63 companies in the technology sector trading on the Montreal and Toronto stock exchanges. With so many potential prospects, the investor's choice becomes more what not to buy than what to buy. By eliminating the obviously undesirable, the investor is left with a much simpler universe to consider.

The Hewlett-Packard Two-Step

Hewlett-Packard goes up and down $6 or $7 dollars every month. I'm in and out of it all the time. I always buy at $52 or lower, and I always sell at $57 or above. And it's working like a dream. The worst case is I end up owning Hewlett-Packard at 50 bucks. It's not a bad deal.

Robert Ferchat, CEO, BCE Mobile Communications

Nineteen-eighty-six marks the beginning of the modern age of technology investing. It was the year Microsoft went public. Before 1986 changes in computer technology were determined by the time between announcements by IBM. At that time, the industry was basically IBM, Digital Equipment Corporation, Hewlett-Packard, Motorola, and a number of large semiconductor companies and small software companies.

The period between 1986 and 1990 was the cowboy stage in technology, The start-up companies were run by technologists, not businessmen. They had no real business model as far as infrastructure, distribution, or channels went. Yet somehow or other, the business miraculously just grew on its own steam. People with ideas moved out of their garages onto the NASDAQ. Professional managers who understood marketing and distribution channels started to take over from the ideas people, and the industry blossomed.

In the early 1990s, institutional investment in technology companies began. In the United States, the technology specialist investment community started to grow, with fund managers, money managers, and analysts — especially those from San Francisco and Boston investment houses — beginning to follow the industry closely. However, it wasn't yet quite important enough to reach the radar screens of the big New York firms. In Canada, all the technology specialists could gather around the same PC terminal.

By 1994, Microsoft, Intel, and Cisco had established their market position and the investment money began to flow. The Internet caught fire and attracted the attention of professional and individual investors who couldn't tell the difference between a transistor and a terminal. Since 1994, venture capitalists have funnelled $5.5 billion into technology start-ups, and the capitalization of the publicly held companies just in and around Silicon Valley approached $500 billion, equal the market value of the entire French stock market. In comparison, the New

York–based financial-services companies are worth $400 billion and the auto industry has a value of barely $100 billion.

The large pension funds, mutual funds, and insurance companies got the technology bug and they all wanted a piece of Microsoft, Intel, and Cisco. As they watched their portfolios grow, they wanted into the smaller companies as well. The momentum players, and those whose trades are based on the benchmark indexes, followed. Suddenly, technology investing was volume trading and volatility city.

Technology Changes at Lightning Speed

Technology is not just the box; it's what's inside. The industry is not only computers and semiconductors. It's the hard disk drive, the power supply, the graphic accelerator, integrated circuits, pro-logic devices, and CAD. It's all the pieces that you can't see, put together by a diverse collection of manufacturers. Following the example of the early auto makers who relied on a pool of skilled suppliers for parts and components, the computer and telecommunications companies count on their network of creative and inventive innovators to rekindle and regenerate themselves.

Investors are prepared to pay a premium for new things. Once things are not that new any more, the premium shrinks and the stocks fall. Then it is on to the next newest thing. In 1994, it was ATM and LAN switching. In 1995, it was semiconductors. In 1996, it was the Internet: Netscape, Spyglass, Netcom, American Online, and UUnet. In 1997, it was Cisco, 3COM, and networking. A glance at the financial charts shows how each fad erupts and then comes crashing down.

The investor always has to bear in mind that what is hot today could be swept aside at any time by emerging competitors and even higher technologies. Product life cycles move so fast that at any time, today's industry darling can be leapfrogged by competitors. The risk of sudden reversals, especially for small companies and those that are counting on a single product, can be catastrophic.

Every decade has its technology trend. In the early 1980s, the information technology industry was propelled by the personal computer revolution, which itself was pushed by spreadsheet and word-processing applications. The killer applications of the 1990s were networking and the Internet. Investors are pondering what trend will dominate the next technology era.

The Next Sensation

I can tell you what's the newest fad right now. It's called Wave Division Multiplexing. Light is a wave length. You take the fibre optic light wave and split it so you get different waves of light and increase the bandwidth. This is the hottest thing right now.

Richard Woo, high-tech analyst,
Thomson Kernaghan & Co. Limited

The Technical Versus the Fundamental Investor

There are two basic approaches to investing in the stock market. The **technical** investor focuses on the action by looking at price movements and trading volumes and applies them to the decision-making process. Technical investors, also called market timers, will also consider commodity prices and general economic indicators such as unemployment, interest rates, inflation, and money supply.

Gary Anderson of Anderson & Loe, a Eugene, Oregon firm that advises money managers, is a typical technical investor. He spends his days with charts, graphs, and data, and pays close attention to the underlying economic environment. "All I'm concerned with is stocks as items which are bought and sold. Price fluctuation is a function of supply and demand," Anderson says. "A stock is a stock is a stock. And the kinds of things that I look for in a technology stock are exactly the kinds of things I look for in a food stock, or anything else."

The **fundamental** investor looks at how a particular stock is doing — its price to earnings ratio, growth potential, etc. Besides studying a corporation's financial data, the fundamental investor will also examine the industry and how the economy will affect the company's core business. Technology investors are generally fundamental investors, making their trades based on the individual performance of the stocks they are following. Of course macroeconomics influences stock performance even in the technology sector, but technology stocks don't always run with the crowd, and neither do technology investors. The one technical factor technology investors do watch carefully is momentum. When technology stocks move, they move fast and furiously. Investors have to be alert so that they get out before it's too late or buy in before they miss their opportunity.

Fundamentally

I'm not a technical person. I don't trade off the charts; I trade off my gut. But I am able to see the group ranking: Is it performing better than its business peers or, at least, in the upper 10 per cent of its peers? Are its earnings per share up this quarter? Those are the kinds of things that can guide you.

From the Experienced Investor

The Old Measuring Stick Doesn't Work Any More

Conventional methods of evaluating mature businesses are left in the horse-and-buggy age when assessing space-age industries. Traditional criteria such as earnings, market share, balance-sheet strength, and momentum are important but don't come close to analysing the intangibles that characterize the digital world. Many of the most interesting technology investment possibilities are still in their early stages of development and haven't yet established themselves sufficiently for these measures to apply.

In other sectors, you can usually evaluate a stock by using these financial factors, but in technology, you have to know the product and the market forces. The stock wouldn't be hot unless the product was hot, so before you appraise the book value, dividend, and yield, you have to evaluate the technology.

How Do You Assess a Future Balance Sheet?

Usually investors look at historical information, current balance-sheet information, and take into account current projections. You can't do that very well with technology. There are so many variables in the market itself: market acceptance, new technology, and leapfrogging. How do you possibly make a projection of what that should look like?

Peter Vanderlee, high-tech entrepreneur, BCD Holdings Inc.

Still, a strong financial picture, with enough available cash and little or no debt, has to be part of the judgement standard. While revenues are often a distant promise, a company has to be judged on its potential, which is a much more uncertain prospect, and potential profits (the returns after expenses have been met) are even less predictable than potential revenues (the total receipts).

"If you are a pulp and paper analyst, you look at the macro level of pricing and availability for wood and the cost per ton for converting it from standing trees to pulp," says Robert MacLellan, Nova Scotia–based technology analyst for New York brokerage, Warburg Dillon Read. "The tech analyst uses the same basic research, but it is focused more on company-specific, company-centric material. You get more into the guts of the actual boxes, and analyse if management makes you comfortable with their strategic outlook. You wrap all these issues together and try and make a judgement call."

"You can't measure in terms of cash flow," says Rick Serafini, manager of the Trimark Discovery Fund, which invests in innovative growth companies. He likes to buy technology companies because they offer him what he calls "forward opportunity." If these companies are successful, he says, he expects them to double their current market capitalization over three to five years, dwarfing their current valuation.

Change Is the Only Constant

Some technology investors are oriented to the very short term, while others are projecting two or three years ahead. For some technologies, the need to change is so crucial that a three-year horizon is an eternity. Others, such as the telephone systems, are like refrigerators — we expect them to be chugging along years from now. To invest in products undergoing huge technological change with a short life cycle, such as software, the range of vision has to be fairly short. For products like telephone systems, where it takes more time to implement change, the investing perspective has to be longer term.

As fast as things are changing, the pace is accelerating even more. One year laptops are the big thing, the next year it's the Windows CE platform for hand-held devices, then, more specifically, the US Robotics Palm Pilot hand-held computer is hot. Smart investors look for companies that can anticipate the changes and have a game plan for moving them forward. Just because a company has a product that's great today, doesn't mean that it will be great three months from now.

Volatility: A Blessing and a Curse

Volatility Index: A Scenario

My definition of volatile is a stock that will fluctuate more than 50 per cent within its 52-week high/low price range. It quickly soars to the moon and just as quickly loses gas and drops off. Let's look at a stock that is trading in the $5–$20 range. In order for me to be interested, it has to go below about $14 because that gives me the 50 per cent fluctuation. Preferably, I would like to see it pull back to about $10 because then, with some further step in the technology, or if a product gets to market, we'll get another run.

Ted Carter, editor of Carter's Choice

If the average portfolio shows an annual gain of 20 per cent, beating most indexes, champagne pours like water. For technology investors, however, that is a minimum. They expect better than that, and a successful technology investment can return well above 100 per cent. It is not unusual for individuals who play in the technology market to expect 10 or 20 times their initial investment. Since the technology stock rally started in November 1992, the benchmark Pacific Stock Exchange technology index has soared 86 per cent a year compared with 26 per cent for the Standard and Poor's 500. More than 10 per cent of all technology stocks doubled or tripled in 1997 despite the October correction. Micron technology was up 147 per cent on the year, Abode Systems was up 106 per cent, and America Online was up 104 per cent. But for investors with less luck and skill, a technology portfolio can be virtually wiped out, leaving them crying in their beer.

The sector is so volatile, it can plunge by 20 per cent, then rocket up again, all within a very short time. When times are good, people are eager to buy, and when things go bad, they are anxious to sell. When the sector stumbles, the decline can easily reach double figures. And when the market hits a significant downturn, as it did in the October 1997 correction, technology stocks lead the tumble even though they are not cyclical.

"The technology market is usually extremely volatile and it is getting worse," says Robert MacLellan of Warburg Dillon Read. "In some sectors, a move of five-eighths or one-half or three-quarters of a point in a day is significant. In the tech market, we expect $2, $3, $4, or $5."

Whether it's general market, technology sector, or individual company–related, that volatility is a fact of the market today. A stock can easily go from $5 to $60 and back to $3. Even Microsoft, selling at $150, cost about $60 just months earlier. Now that's real volatility.

There is, of course, no way to completely eliminate risk in what is, in essence, a high-risk investment. But with diligence, attentiveness, setting limits on the maximum loss, and keeping within certain boundaries, you can minimize the risk. "The level of diligence goes beyond what a conventional investor might need to do," says Brian Ashford-Russell of the Mackenzie Universal World Science and Technology Fund. "Investing in technology is similar to investing in any other industry, but the pace of change is much faster. Therefore, you have to be much more conscious of the development of competitive changes in market position and more fluid in your decisions."

As volatile as the entire technology stock industry is, some stocks are more risky than others. Typically small-cap companies are more risky than large-cap companies which have the resources to ride the up and down cycles. Speculators in early-stage technology companies sometimes have to suffer through several duds before striking it rich, but patience can pay off. When success strikes, it can mean a big score. In the mining sector, a mine can be dry and the investors will stick with the mining promoter. Investors patiently stayed with Murray Pezim through several duds before he struck it rich with the Hemlo mine which became the biggest gold find in Canada. "The real hallmark is that investors have to take this exciting package of growth and opportunity and confusion and volatility all together," says Benn Mikula, technology analyst for RBC Dominion Securities Inc.

Risky Business

You're not investing in stability. That's the investment premise. Growth is by nature risky and the risk of not hitting targets, the risks of things going badly, and managers not often running businesses well are often enormous. You look at the components of this risk and you try to chisel away at them as best you can.

Loudon Owen, venture capitalist, McLean Watson Capital Inc.

The volatility is almost a self-fulfilling prophecy. People expect to see wild swings in stocks, so they behave in ways that magnify the problem. The more people are convinced that the stocks are going to have a wild swing, the more they sell or buy into it. This attracts momentum investors trying to cash in on the volatility. They buy and sell based on how rapidly and how drastically prices change regardless of value. Momentum investors add even more volatility to the sector, making it even more exciting.

"The volatility comes because these are growth stocks," says Alex Batula, software analyst at Midland Walwyn Capital Inc. "You pay for growth stocks what you think they will be worth a few years from now. The perception of what they can earn can change, which accounts for the volatility. You may want to separate volatility from risk. Microsoft is more volatile than General Motors but doesn't present any more risk."

Alex Batula makes clear this distinction between risk and volatility, as do other stock market experts. Risk refers to the danger that you will lose all or part of your investment, while volatility refers to the rapid and extreme fluctuations in price. Volatility terms, like standard deviation and beta, come close to reflecting our perception of risk. Beta expresses how much a stock or fund fluctuates relative to the market as a whole, while standard deviation describes how much an investment's monthly performance has strayed from its average return.

Dr. Chuck Chakrapani, Toronto-based editor of *Money Digest*, a journal of investing and personal finance, enjoys the challenge of investing in technology stocks. He tries to use the sector's volatility to cut his risk and maximize his returns by buying and selling nimbly. "If a stock loses 20 per cent, I get out. I don't care, I can always get back in later. When it goes up, I have a sell philosophy as well. I'll buy a thousand shares and if it goes up 10 or 12 per cent, I'll sell a hundred. If it keeps going up, I'll sell another hundred. So I keep watching and selling as it keeps going up. But you must be prepared to take losses because you have to be in and out."

Risk Is In the Eye of the Beholder

The risk in technology investments is very overstated. I agree there's a very high risk specific to technology stocks, but a portfolio of them gives you tremendous diversification, particularly if that diversification is geographical as well as on a cross-industry basis.

Brian Ashford-Russell, co-manager,
Mackenzie Universal World Science and Technology Fund

The Similarities Between Technology and Mining Stocks

Words of Wisdom

In mining you're exploiting the earth; in technology you are exploiting the human mind.

John Drolet, analyst, Yorkton Securities Inc.

Although technology acts like no other sector of the market, if people want a parallel, they could look to the mining sector. The most glaring similarity is that both are highly volatile, with new companies offering an opportunity based on an idea or a belief that something needs to be developed. In reality, maybe one in a thousand exploration programs results in a working mine, which is about the same ratio as technology ideas becoming commercially viable.

When you own a piece of land, you set the pace of exploration. It is your decision when to dig. But in the technology business, you don't have that luxury. The life cycle for products is short, the competition global, and the pace of change so rapid that you cannot sit on an idea, like a mining claim, and treat it as an asset. You have to start investing as quickly as you can in research and development, or somebody else will beat you to the punch.

Ted Carter is the editor of *Carter's Choice*, a newsletter for market players, and author of *Successful Stock Market Speculation*. He calls himself a trader and not an investor. An investor, he says, puts money into a company looking for long-term growth, while as a trader he is following the day-to-day swings of the stock. Because of their volatility, Carter finds the technology and mining areas most rewarding. He says the confidence factor or investor sentiment matter most in these sectors. The excitement surrounding both technology and mining stocks depends on an idea or a dream. A stock will rise and fall depending on how much people believe in that dream. Ironically, once the company enters the stage of successfully realizing the real potential of the product or site, the excitement for the stock dies down for the average investor. Justifiably or not, keenness about the stock's prospects dwindles.

"Good ideas tend to run a stock up. If the idea does not come to fruition, it crashes. Stocks run higher on anticipation of good results than they ever do when the find or prospect is eventually turned into a mine. Once you get into the development stage, the stock becomes very boring." Ted Carter means boring in the stock market sense; it doesn't have the same dynamic swings or volume any more.

There's always a certain amount of luck involved, says First Marathon biotechnology analyst Cameron Groome. "Everybody has a little chuckle about the cheap mining promoter suddenly becoming a genius once he finds a mine. Meanwhile, all the guys that didn't find mines are still cheap mining promoters. It is similar in the biotech area where the guy who got lucky is suddenly brilliant, and the guy who didn't get lucky was a bum all along."

Stages of Development

The How to Beat Them Blues

It's easy to go into a technology business, it's staying in business that's tough.

One of the riskiest, and at the same time most lucrative, investments in technology is in young start-up companies. A way to assess the risk factor is to recognize the stages of development a technology company goes through. Because the pace of development has to be so rapid to beat the competition, the cycle is accelerated and the stages are more clearly defined. The typical cycle for a successful start-up technology company is two years. In the first stage of the cycle, the company develops its product, usually with venture capital funds. In the next stage, the product is available for market and the stock is ready for the stock market. In the third stage, the product is either a success in the market place, or it isn't. By this time, the technology company can be considered to be mature. It will have captured the attention of competitors who can copy the product and sell it for less, or, in the case of a large competitor, acquire the company. Before those two years are up, the company had better be working on its next product. You have to be sure that the company you are investing in has a strategy to protect itself by upgrading its product or by inventing a new one.

It is easy enough to reverse-engineer most technologies. Patents and copyright laws are vague enough that most things can be copied at far less cost than inventing them from scratch. Once the same technology is offered by more than one source, since mark-ups are so high, competition brings the price down astronomically and affects the profitability of the company and its stock price. Before a product is actually ready to go to market, the stock price can soar. But many times, the ideas look good just on paper and when the commercial product is finally ready, nobody wants it and it turns out to be a bust. "You have to remember that the type of people that are in that technology business tend to be blue-sky-type geniuses and do not give a lot of thought sometimes to 'Does the market want or need this,'" says speculator Ted Carter.

The investor who likes the challenge and the potential reward of a risky and volatile investment can jump on the roller coaster at any time in its run. There is nothing like a start-up technology company for the thrills and bumps of speculation. Any time in the two-year development period you can experience the gut-wrenching low of a dip or the exhilarating high of a surge. With a start-up, sometimes it is better to be in and out before the product is actually produced. The market counts on demand and if the product doesn't meet the demand projections, the price of the stock will plunge.

One theory suggests that new technology is all about monopoly. As a new product is invented, the company responsible, in effect, creates a demand for that product and has the monopoly to meet that demand. The rise and fall of the underlying equity depends on the company's ability to maintain that monopoly by capturing and protecting the market from its competitors. Then the company has to develop a new invention to maintain claim to that monopoly, or it erodes and the cycle begins again.

Delrina Corporation is a good example. It came to market with WinFax, a fax modem program for Microsoft Windows. With its monopoly, Delrina was able sell four million copies. By the time Microsoft incorporated a fax modem program into Windows 95, Delrina was already negotiating the sale of the company to Symantec. WinFax still exists, but now as a minor player in the fax modem market, not with the stranglehold it once had. In the Delrina-Microsoft showdown, Microsoft was interested in the strategic value of having the fax modem software as part of its operating system and less in the profits that could accrue. Microsoft is employing the same strategy in its confrontation with Netscape over the Web browser market. For the time being, it's market share that counts. Profits will follow.

It's a matter of simple microeconomics. Credible competitors in a market have a significant impact on rates of growth of a company and risk in an investment by introducing pricing pressure. An agile company strikes before the competition gets too hot. Intel brings out a new generation of semiconductor every couple of years, or less. IBM, Compaq, and Dell beef up their product lines every six months to a year. For companies to be successful in the technology environment, the upgrades have to be fast and frequent. Each and every cycle, they have to be prepared to address the demands of the market with products which are readily available and priced in an attractive way.

Riding the Cycles

In every speculative stock, you always have the excitement of a new thing happening. Stocks spurt up on news, and then drift down on no news. That is when the real boring selling starts. The volume gets very thin because even the late trailers want to go where there's excitement and activity. Then the stock doesn't have a spike down; it just drifts down. The sharp spikes occur when something has gone wrong during the R&D and they find out, "Hey, this isn't going to work," or when they get the product to market and find out, "Hey, this isn't going to sell."

Ted Carter, editor of Carter's Choice

Business Cycles

Steel, airlines, and energy are cyclic products, or commodities, which do better during a strong economic upturn, and suffer disproportionately in an economic downturn. Technology and other growth stocks grow faster than the economy as a whole. This natural upward bias actually reduces long-term volatility, and technology remains relatively immune to business cycles. "Over a 10-year view, you're probably better off owning a basket of high-quality growth stocks than a basket of cyclical stocks," says Benn Mikula, high-tech analyst for RBC Dominion. "The demand for corporate communications and computer networks will not disappear in the next recession, so you have more protection in a down economy."

The Big One

We've mentioned the cycle of growth of a company as it matures. We have also mentioned the cycle of the stock market as it ebbs and flows with spikes and dips. The cycle that worries a lot of investors is the Big One. Many influential and respected people — bears — believe despair and gloom in the stock market are inevitable. These market sceptics say the market is overheated and the boom can't go on forever. So far, the doomsters are the ones who have been embarrassed. A lot of investors in technology have never experienced a down, or bear, market. The market, especially technology, has been so good for so long.

"I've never been around in a bear market. I don't know what a bear market is," says technology investor Allan Blatt. "Is a bear market six days, six weeks, six months, or six years? I think maybe all of the above. I think tech stocks had a hell of a correction earlier this year. Many stocks were down 10 to 20 per cent off their highs. Could that have been the bear market? Had

I listened to every naysayer for the last three years, where would I be? Part of it is blind optimism — I want it to be great. But as I look at the demographics, I see how much money is flooding into mutual funds and realize fund managers are paid to put money to work. I don't know when the party is going to end."

If the bubble bursts, will it blow up overnight, or will there be a slow, steady leakage over time? This question has real implications for the technology investor. If the leakage is slow, then there is the opportunity of getting out while the getting is good. But if the bubble bursts overnight, there is the prospect of being stuck with empty pockets and chewing gum all over a lot of sad faces. The bulls — and most technology followers are bulls — say the crash is never going to happen. They point to other down cycles and show how technology has always rallied. Even in a recession, they say, technology stocks are insulated. There is no question that there have been scares. When the big technology companies, Hewlett-Packard and Motorola most notably, have reported less than stellar quarters and their stocks were hit, they dragged the market down with them. But optimistic investors always see this as a buying opportunity and it doesn't take long for a rebound.

During the last lengthy rally, the technology market has been led by large-cap stocks such as Microsoft, Cisco, and Intel. Meanwhile the small- and medium-cap stocks have performed less well, and nobody knows if and when there will be a correction, but the thinking goes that if there is one, the small caps will come around. The smart investors have already protected themselves by diversifying, holding both large- and small-cap technology stocks in their portfolio.

The technology industry has been on a roll since 1992 with no real sign of abating. The computer boom of the late 1970s, which started with the emergence of Apple, lasted until the mid-1980s. The 1970s' boom was fuelled by companies focused heavily on single products, either computers or semiconductors. The 6000

An Optimistic View

The sector will continue to regenerate itself because there will always be something new. Everything is about speed. That's the main thing that drives this industry...speed. As long as you produce things that are faster...you'll continue to sell.

Richard Woo, high-tech analyst,
Thomson Kernaghan & Co. Limited

new technology companies, with total sales of $200 billion, cover a diverse maze of industries, including hardware, software, networking, and semiconductors, and account for 10 per cent of the American gross domestic product. The evolution of these new companies is decentralized, allowing them to spawn new ideas and other companies. Economists call this approach to business flexible recycling — with old concepts being allowed to die and new ones to emerge — allowing ideas, people, and capital to be reallocated. An essential ingredient in this new paradigm is the investor recognizing and financing new opportunities.

As we will learn in the next chapter, before investors focusing on the technology sector specifically can identify which of these opportunities will be financially rewarding, it pays to understand how the stock market works generally. Although it is true that technology market marches to its own drummer the beat is set by the rhythm of the market as a whole.

PLAY BY THE RULES

Greed motivates, greed at times pays off, but it is greed, pure and simple, that leads most investors into making their biggest mistakes.

Gordon Gekko, Wall Street

Stock market investors are all after the same thing: to buy low and sell high. No matter what rules or formulas they follow, they are looking for that edge that will allow them to spot a stock when it's a bargain and sell it for as big a profit as they can. This basic principle of investing transcends all others, no matter what the sector.

Discipline is the key when buying stocks. Normally cautious investors may be motivated by greed when they see a lot of other players making a killing on a particular speculative stock. The basic principles that made them smart investors suddenly go by the board. And while throwing out the rule book and jumping on the bandwagon may pay off sometimes, there is always the risk of a fiasco. Being a good investor is like being a good baseball pitcher. You can't get too upset when you blow one, and you can't get too excited when you blow them away.

One accepted investment strategy is to buy and hold: forget about the short-term fluctuations and hang in for the long term. Another legitimate tactic is to speculate that the stock will do well over the short term. Of course every investor has his or her own definition of what short or long term means. Some speculators — day traders, for example — will trade on an uptick or downtick within a single day. That takes close attention and a lot of luck. For other speculators, short term can mean months.

In the technology sector, there are many examples of both long- and short-term success stories. Silicon Graphics went up 34 per cent on good news on one sunshiny day. But a short-term success cycle in technology is usually two years and is characterized by small, single-product companies with good ideas and really good timing that show dramatic revenue growth. Some of the Internet companies like Spyglass had good short-term runs. A long-term cycle success occurs when a company is able to capture the market for its product so completely that the competition can never catch up. Microsoft, Intel, and Cisco are legitimate long-term successes.

Ten Basic Must Dos

The 10 basic must dos are:

1. Diversify

2. Buy low

3. Set a maximum loss limit

4. Don't fall in love with a stock

5. Don't "chase" fast-rising stocks

6. Beware of "tips" and rumours

7. Take note of who is promoting the stock

8. Get solid facts

9. Don't go into debt to buy stocks

10. Be aware of cycles

1. Diversify: Don't Put All Your Eggs in One Basket

The most important rule is to diversify by buying different sectors. Technology is a speculative sector with a lot of risk, and it is useful to remind yourself that technology stocks are a value-added part of your portfolio, not the entire portfolio. Even within the technology portion of a portfolio, you can hedge by diversifying among different subsectors like hardware, software, and telecommunications. Another way to balance your portfolio is by buying stocks with a large capitalization, as well as those with a small capitalization. When large caps fall out of favour, the market tends to swing towards small caps and vice versa. You can also balance those stocks you plan to hold for the long term with those you plan to trade. This tip will be discussed in greater detail later in this chapter.

2. Buy Low

Professional investors talk about stocks being undervalued, fully valued, or overvalued. Undervalued means that when you assess the worth of the stock, there is room for growth. A stock may be undervalued because its earnings history is inconsistent, or because the company is not well known. Try to identify undervalued corporate stocks to invest in before they become fully valued. Undervalued companies are often takeover targets because acquiring companies can buy the assets inexpensively. A security is said to be overvalued when its price is not justified by its price to earnings ratio, or is out of line with the rest of the industry, and thus should eventually decline. Microsoft, trading at about

$150, is considered to be undervalued by some investors. Buying low does not mean buying a penny stock and praying.

3. Set a Maximum Loss Limit

When you buy a stock, you can give your broker a stop-loss order. If the price falls below a certain dollar value, or drops more than an agreed percentage, the stock is automatically sold. Many investors choose 20 per cent as a nice round stop-loss measure which can create a flurry of activity. That's why it is wise to choose an odd number like 19 or 21 per cent so that you don't get stopped out too soon or too late. A loss has to be measured not only in absolute dollar terms, but also in terms of the money that could have been invested somewhere else. (See Chapter 6: When to Sell.)

4. Don't Fall in Love with a Stock

This is the tip that is most closely tied to greed. Be rational about your investment and smart enough to recoup your investment instead of trying to ride the wave of a stock until the very last crest. "Leave something for the needy and greedy" is the credo of the wise investor. If you are too greedy, you may come out of the situation with nothing.

5. Don't "Chase" Fast-Rising Stocks

Stocks are built on confidence. Their value shoots up when investors flood their money into an idea. To follow these trends without an understanding of the company's fundamentals can be a recipe for disaster.

6. Beware of "Tips" and Rumours

If it's hot talk around the office water-cooler, chances are you've already missed the boat. By the time the information reaches you, the insiders have already made their profit and are looking to get out before the stock falls. If a stock has moved up recently on increasing trading volume, it's a sure sign that many others heard the rumour before you did. You risk being the last one to jump aboard before the bandwagon crashes.

7. Take Note of Who Is Promoting the Stock

Reputation is crucial in the investment industry. The experience and integrity of the people behind the company are as important, if not more so, as the claims that they state and the papers they circulate about the stock issue. Do your homework.

8. Get Solid Facts

A company should be willing to share any information with a potential investor. Any hesitancy to provide such information should be a sure-fire sign that something is wrong. Remember, speculative stocks are based primarily on an idea, and faith in that idea. Ask all the questions you possibly can to make the idea become more tangible.

9. Don't Go into Debt to Buy Stocks

With speculative stocks, it is not advisable to borrow from your broker, or anyone else, in order to buy the latest new issue. When you do this, you are gambling, not investing. The volatility index is far too high to chance financial disaster. If you don't have it, don't spend it.

10. Be Aware of Cycles

In all stocks, there are seasonal cycles which the investor should be aware of. With technology stocks, R&D cycles can be tracked. For example, summer is not the best time to buy. In each of the past three years, share prices ended the summer about where they began. There are several reasons for the summer slowdown: Many investors have invested their tax-return money by the end of May; as is the case in other industries, most portfolio managers take their vacations in midsummer and this causes the exchange to slow down significantly; announcements of major advancements usually happen towards late summer.

John Drolet's Rules

1. You have to be patient.
2. You have to be careful.
3. You shouldn't fall in love with a company. The market has no room for emotion.
4. Look at a company's prospects and decide whether it's worthwhile to invest in it.
5. You have to have a diversified portfolio, so don't put all your resources into one company. Spread it around.

John Drolet, high-tech analyst, Yorkton Securities

Ten Basic Don't Dos

The 10 basic don't dos are:

1. Purchase last year's winner

2. Follow others into a "hot stock"

3. Believe that a stock will not bounce back after it falls

4. Make other people's mistakes

5. Misread analysts

6. Look only at company earnings

7. Take chances on new issues (IPOs)

8. Fall in love with a stock

9. Change strategies in mid-course

10. Bite off more than you can chew

1. Purchase Last Year's Winner

Although it is advisable to examine a company's historical performance, the past is not necessarily indicative of future results. If we apply the two-year formula of development, last year's winner might have reached the extent of its extreme growth.

2. Follow Others into a "Hot Stock"

The key is anticipating — getting in early and having others follow you.

3. Believe That a Stock Will Not Bounce Back after It Falls

Newer stocks, especially technology stocks, are extremely volatile. A safe stop-loss order on technology stocks can be as high as 27 per cent compared to 15 per cent for other less volatile stocks. So pick and stick. A commonly used stock market theory, the Dead Cat Bounce, is more applicable to technology stocks than any other sector. The Dead Cat Bounce theory describes a stock's tendency to have a short-term rebound immediately following a significant pullback. These rebounds seem to occur even if the pull back was caused by bad news. The rationale is that no matter how dead a cat is, if you slam it against the ground hard enough, it's bound to bounce a little.

4. Make Other People's Mistakes

Do your own research. One key to success in the stock market, especially in the technology sector, is to do your homework. Verify whatever you hear.

5. Misread Analysts

Analysts' reports, while carefully researched, are couched in very careful language and often don't include a time horizon for an investment. (See Chapter 3.)

6. Look Only at Company Earnings

Revenue growth and market share should be considered when making a decision.

7. Take Chances on New Issues (IPOs)

The typical IPO gains 11 per cent on the first day, then starts nosing down after the first week. It takes about a year and a half for the early buyers and speculators to move on and for the stock price to stabilize.

8. Fall in Love with a Stock

If a stock's performance is not meeting your expectations, there is no shame in letting it go. (See Chapter 6, "When To Sell.")

9. Change Strategies in Mid-Course

Decide whether you are in for the short, intermediate, or long term and stick to your plan.

10. Bite Off More Than You Can Chew

Make sure you understand how much risk you are prepared to take. If you are always concerned that you won't have enough money for future obligations, these stocks may be too uncertain for you. If you constantly worry about whether you made a mistake when you purchase items like clothing, furniture, or computers, you might not have the stomach for the vagaries of this market.

Diversify: The First and Most Important Must Do

Even a crap shooter would be a fool to bet the number seven every time. So unless you have ice water in your veins, you want some variety in your portfolio. Nobody can say what the proper proportion of technology should be. It depends on the individual's tolerance for risk, stage of life, and how the market is performing at a given time.

One way to cut the risk is through diversification. By owning a bundle of stocks, you are smoothing the uncertainty. Nobody can pick stocks with enough pinpoint accuracy to hit the target every time. The ultimate bundling is a mutual fund where the fund manager balances the portfolio. How much is in a bundle? Academics say that mathematically you achieve complete diversification in the stock market with only eight stocks. But if you consider the risk to be twice as high in the technology sector, which is a reasonable assumption, you might consider a bundle of perhaps 16 stocks. However, diversifying too much negates the whole principle of taking enough risk to outperform the market. You might as well buy an index fund that matches a broad-based index such as the S&P 500. An index fund achieves the same return as the general market.

Diversifying within the technology sector is more than possible. The technology sector is not a monolith but a continuum made up of segments that act independently. Part 2 of this book will give you an insight into the individual trading characteristics of the subsectors — hardware and computers; semiconductors and microchips; computer peripherals; software; networking and the Internet; entertainment and media; the wireless world; and biotechnology — and how they interact. The semiconductor sector moves first, followed by computer hardware and equipment, and then by the softer technologies. Choosing a cross-section of subsectors cushions your investments. You can also balance large-cap stocks with small-cap stocks. Most observers find that when the large caps are hot, the small caps are not. You can also balance safer mature companies with riskier newer issues.

Diversifying your portfolio is the best way to cut risk. By focusing on the performance of your portfolio as a whole rather than constantly watching one stock or another, you increase your chances. Nobody is suggesting balancing winners with dogs. May all your picks be stars. But the reality is that technology is a risky sector. While some stocks will be doing well, others may not. The more your portfolio is diversified, the less likely it is that you will lose it all.

You can get tremendous diversity within technology. Maybe the wildest software companies that have no earnings are too scary for you. Maybe you would rather have AT&T which has great earnings and value. Maybe you want Microsoft, the greatest name in software. Maybe their multiple is too high so you can go for IBM at 14 times earnings. Maybe smaller companies that fall somewhere between those low and high multiples are more your style. You have to play to your strength. If you know you are a nervous investor, you want to be sure your exposure is in lower multiple, less volatile technology companies.

Jonathan Steinberg, publisher and editor, Individual Investor

Big and Small

One of the methods of diversification we explored in the last section is holding both large-cap and small-cap companies in your portfolio. Capitalization refers to the price of the stock multiplied by the number of shares. Microsoft, the company with the second-largest capitalization in the world, has 1.3 billion shares issued, at $135 a share, and has a market capitalization of $180 billion. Large-cap companies, usually identified as those with a total market value of $5 billion or more, tend to have a more predictable rate of growth and offer more resistance to price decline during down markets. The chances of the solid ones — like Microsoft and IBM — collapsing are the same as any other blue chip stock faltering. Small-cap companies, with a total market value of $1 billion or less, achieve more rapid growth but when markets go down, their prices fall more than average. Micro-cap stocks, with a market value of $100 million or less, are characterized by high volatility, illiquidity, and wide spreads between the bid and ask prices. While technology investing is by definition high-risk investing, when you pick small young companies, you are being exceptionally speculative.

If you pick a bundle of 10 solid companies it doesn't matter if three or four falter; the others will make up for the difference, says Chuck Chakrapani, editor of *Money Digest*. But at the bottom end, it's hard to know how many will survive. "I would divide the market into two basic categories," he says. "If you want technology for the future, then you invest in solid, major stocks. IBM, Oracle, and Microsoft are buy and holds. If you want to make money out of volatility, then invest in smaller, less-established companies and treat it as a unique investment opportunity with lots of risk."

One accepted rule of thumb in the market is that small caps and large caps operate as mirror images of each other. It bears repeating that when large caps are hot, as they are now, small caps lag. And when the large caps cool down, the small caps forge ahead.

The Bigger, the Better

With large well-established companies, you know there will always be buyers willing to step up to the plate if you need to unload quickly, so there is never a concern about liquidity. Smaller-cap firms have a narrower investor base, and you might have a tougher time selling your holdings at a reasonable price. Also, large institutions, mutual funds, and pension funds tend to support large companies. These investors are usually in for the long haul and, on the whole, are more risk-averse. Individual investors concerned about risk can follow what the institutions are doing. There is safety in numbers.

For all these reasons, larger caps tend to be less volatile. They are not likely to lose half their market value overnight on bad news, which is always a possibility with the smaller companies. Over the last two years, larger-cap technology stocks have far outperformed the market as a whole and small-cap technology has been one of the worst performing areas of the market. "One truth of the market is that a basket of well-known names will stand you in good stead. You won't get sunk if one particular one gets hit by a torpedo," says Benn Mikula, head of technology research at RBC Dominion Securities Inc. "If you had held a basket of Lucent, Northern Telecom, and Newbridge, or IBM, Microsoft, Intel, and Cisco, you would have done phenomenally well for the last two years."

Small Is Beautiful

Track record is the best prediction of future performance. If I were betting on a big technology company, I expect their track record is going to be more or less the same as it has been in the past. If I'm betting on a small company, then I would sure as hell want to make my bets small.

Robert Ferchat, CEO, BCE Mobile Communications

Some investors protect themselves by only buying the leaders in a sector — like Microsoft, Intel, and Cisco — because these large-cap companies can weather competition, and through dominance and market share catch up quickly. "Established companies often have the resources to crush the little guys," says Franklin Resources money manager Edward Jamieson. "That's what we always worry about with the little new start-ups. We do invest in start-ups, but we are very careful to make sure that they can carve a niche out for themselves that is big enough for them to grow into."

Large-cap companies also tend to have more extensive product lines that shelter them if one product stumbles. But even that is changing. Reflecting the volatility of the stock market as a whole, even in this good market the large caps are subject to drastic ups and downs, mostly with dramatic increases. But when things go wrong, they can go desperately wrong. "What I have been noticing is that the tendency for stability is getting less and less," says Robert MacLellan. "If you look at Nortel over the last six months, its volatility has gone through the roof relative to a year ago. Like every other stock, if they go up fast, they can go down even faster. God help them if they have a disappointing quarter." In the correction of October 1997, Northern Telecom was one of the hardest hit.

Richard Woo, high-tech analyst for Thomson Kernaghan & Co. Limited, a Toronto firm that follows and likes small-cap companies, says individual investors are not saddled by the same restrictive market capitalization criteria the institutional investors are. "If you want to get a bigger bang for the buck, you want to find the next big winners," he says. "There are a lot of smaller companies coming out with new technologies. You are taking additional risk, of course, but that's what's called growth potential."

Money manager Jonathan Steinberg, the publisher and editor of the American personal finance magazine *Individual Investor*, made his reputation picking small stocks with rapid growth and exciting new products. He cautions that you have to work harder to make yourself familiar with all the financial details of a company that might not be as closely followed as a large cap. But if you do your homework well, there is a better chance of finding a sleeper among the small caps that the institutional investors have missed.

"There are 8000 companies traded publicly on the NYSE, AMEX, and NASDAQ and 70 per cent of them have market caps under $250 million," he says. "I think these are particularly poorly followed, so there is a lot of opportunity there. Our research tells us that our 450,000 readers put in 15 to 20 hours of investment research a week."

Brian Ashford-Russell, head of technology investing for Henderson Investors in London, England and co-manager of the Mackenzie Universal World Science and Technology Fund, says the approach to investing in a young company is very different from the way you would think about a developed technology. "If you intend to be an investor in Blue Sky Technology Company, your tolerance for risk must be 100 per cent."

By their very nature, large-cap technology companies tend to have large international sales forces. In a low-interest-rate environment, as we are experiencing now, there is a strong export orientation, so these large companies do well. Smaller-cap companies do well when interest rates are higher or when we are coming out of a bad stock market. But with smaller companies today increasingly generating overseas sales earlier in their life cycles, the export gap between large-cap companies and small-cap companies is narrowing.

No one size fits all seasons. When big cap loses favour, then it's the small companies that have relative value and significantly outperform the big companies.

Ian Ainsworth, fund manager,
Altamira Science and Technology Fund

NASDAQ

If you are going to invest in technology, you have to know about NASDAQ, the National Association of Securities Dealers Automated Quotation System. NASDAQ is the home of high-tech stocks and any serious technology investor has to trade on it. Established in 1971, NASDAQ didn't have too much respectability even 10 years ago. But today, the fact that technology stocks trade there almost exclusively has made it world renowned. Since all the most important foreign technology stocks are cross-traded on their home exchange and NASDAQ, it lists close to 6000 domestic and foreign companies, more than any other stock market in the world. NASDAQ gives the investor access to practically every major technology stock in the world, and it is the dream of every technology company anywhere in the world to go public on NASDAQ to reach American investors as quickly as possible. NASDAQ's share volume reached 138.1 billion shares in 1996 and dollar volume reached $3.3 trillion. In 1996, NASDAQ share volume surpassed all other US stock markets.

NASDAQ: A Little Background

In 1982, 63 per cent of all shares changing hands traded on the New York Stock Exchange (NYSE), while NASDAQ accounted for 32 per cent. But by 1992, NASDAQ's share of the market jumped to 47 per cent while the Big Board dwindled to 50 per cent. The former two-for-cne lead has turned into a dead heat, and although the NYSE retains a big lead in dollar volume, it is losing that lead as well.

NASDAQ is not a place. Unlike the New York Stock Exchange, there are no shouting, gesticulating traders thronging its floor, because it has no floor. NASDAQ is an association of Market Maker firms tied together by telephones and computers. Because the stocks on NASDAQ have so much volume, they are easy to trade and follow.

NASDAQ and
Technology Companies

Technology companies want to trade on NASDAQ because it's an opportunity for them to raise capital quickly, build their public profile, and get liquidity. Listing requirements are less stringent for NASDAQ than for the more established exchanges, such as NYSE, so it is attractive for fast-growing smaller companies.

NASDAQ is well covered by analysts and is on the radar screen of other companies. That's critical because technology is a business of alliances. NASDAQ has become the financial crossroads of the public technology community. Technology companies, both public and private, watch it closely because the ups and the downs of NASDAQ give them an indication of what their competitors, clients, suppliers, and partners are doing. At first NASDAQ was an exchange where investors looked for risky issues, like the Vancouver Stock Exchange (VSE) or the Alberta Stock Exchange (ASE) are in Canada. Over time, the risks have started to settle down and the exchange has become much more balanced. Microsoft, Cisco, and Intel are still loyal to their NASDAQ roots.

McLean Watson Capital Inc. venture capitalist Loudon Owen and his partner John Eckert encourage their Canadian portfolio companies to consider NASDAQ when they are ready to go public. One of their investments, 3D graphics software company SOFTIMAGE Inc., was the first Quebec company to go public on NASDAQ. Despite the cultural challenges and regulatory costs, it was an enormous success for the company, giving it the extensive investor support and clout it needed. "At first companies were tarnished by being listed on NASDAQ," says Owen. "Now NASDAQ is comparable to the more senior exchanges for credibility, level of surveillance, and consistent regulatory practices."

How NASDAQ Works

What distinguishes NASDAQ is its use of computers and a vast telecommunications network to create an electronic trading system that allows market participants to meet over the computer rather than face to face. It is also known as the Over-the-Counter

(OTC) market since stocks trade over the counter with multiple Market Makers ready to buy or sell a specific stock, even if nobody else bids for it. In an auction market like the New York and the Toronto stock exchanges, brokers act strictly as go-betweens.

The Over-the-Counter market actually has three tiers. The best capitalized and most active OTC stocks are NASDAQ National Market Issues. The listing requirements to be included in this group are relatively stringent, including an independent board of directors, annual shareholder meetings, shareholder approval to issue additional shares, and prohibitions against shareholder disenfranchisement.

The companies in the second tier, listed under NASDAQ Small-Cap Issues, are considerably less capitalized with fewer assets and revenues, fewer shares outstanding, and a lower price per share. The stocks in this group are extremely speculative. The lowest-level non-NASDAQ stocks are listed on the Pink Sheets published each business day by the National Quotation Bureau and distributed to brokerage firms. These are low-priced and thinly traded. Since there is no central reporting, day-to-day prices have to be obtained directly from the Market Makers.

Over 500 member firms act as NASDAQ Market Makers. The typical NASDAQ stock has 11 Market Makers actively competing with one another to post the best quotes by displaying buy and sell quotations for a guaranteed number of shares. Once an order is received, the Market Maker will immediately purchase shares for, or sell shares from, its own inventory.

An important component of each quote is how many shares the Market Maker is prepared to fill at that particular price, called "size of the market." The implication for the individual investor is that the Market Makers are more prepared to fill large orders than small ones. So while the price you are offering to acquire a stock might be higher than another offer, you won't get to purchase it at that price if the size of the market is bigger for the other offer. In an auction market, if you bid the higher price, you get the order no matter how many shares you are willing to buy or sell.

This led, in the past, to allegations of unfair trading practices. When the brokerage firm acts as an agent or go-between, it simply arranges the trade between buyer and seller, and charges a commission for its services. When the brokerage acts as a Market Maker, or dealer/principal, it's either buying or selling from its own account (to or from the customer). The customers are charged either a mark-up or a mark-down, depending on whether they are buying or selling. While the brokerage is prohibited from charging both a mark-up (or mark-down) and a commission, dealers/principals are not necessarily required to disclose the amount of the mark-up or mark-down. There were complaints that the spreads between the bid/ask prices were too high, providing Market Makers with returns far outstripping those their clients were getting. The spread is the difference between the price at which a Market Maker is willing to buy a security and the price at which he is prepared to sell.

The National Association of Security Dealers (NASD), which regulates NASDAQ, has been taking measures to protect stockholders in these transactions and to improve fairness. In 1996, NASD opened the Office of Individual Investor Services to serve as the individual investors' advocate. Now Market Makers must be able to display that they made every effort to obtain the best posted price for their clients.

Academic research has shown that an auction market such as the NYSE results in tighter ranges in price between trades and less volatility. However, the NASDAQ model makes sure that the trading is active and volumes stay high. Despite the NASDAQ requirement of making a market, during the crash of 1987 the NYSE performed much better in keeping the market active. Many OTC Market Makers simply stopped answering their phones until the dust settled.

Investors can now trade NASDAQ options. The NASDAQ 100 Index reflects the largest growth companies across major industry groups listed on the exchange. These companies have a market capitalization of at least $500 million and a daily average trading volume of at least 100,000 shares. The NASDAQ 100 Index began trading on the Chicago Board Options Exchange in 1994 and the Chicago Mercantile Exchange in 1996.

NASDAQ claims its computerized trading system is more efficient and just as fair as the Big Board's auction system with its flesh-and-blood specialists. NASDAQ says it is the home for companies of the future, implying that the Big Board is for the tired old giants.

Buying Internationally

The United States is the world leader in technology, and Silicon Valley is the engine that drives it. That small region south of San Francisco in northern California is home to one-fifth of the world's top 100 high-tech companies, with the top five boasting combined revenues of $40 billion and a market capitalization over $250 billion. Boston, Austin (Texas), Raleigh-Durham (North Carolina) and Seattle — home of Microsoft — are also high-tech centres. Talent from around the world flocks to Silicon Valley. One-third of its engineers were born outside the United States and the multicultural flavour reaches to the highest ranks of the most important companies. With the entrepreneurial spirit as the key to the growth of the region, Silicon Valley has a critical mass of brainpower, a well-integrated supplier base, and financial backing.

In the United States, technology is a research-driven sector. The real challenge for the North American technology investors is to sort through the research and figure out how much is salesmanship and how much is real. The challenge is equally as large for global investors, but it's different. In most countries, technology is under-researched. But with the opportunities at home well picked over, American investors are looking around the world for other opportunities. Some Canadian technology companies, especially telecommunications and networking companies based in Canada's Silicon Valley North in and around Ottawa — like Newbridge Networks — are cross-listed on Canadian exchanges and NASDAQ, and are getting attention from American investors and analysts. At the same time, the Canadian investment community is looking towards the United States where there is more choice, risk, and rewards.

Canadian and American stock markets function in much the same ways, and investors on either side of the border can trade on exchanges in both countries with hardly any differentiation, except for exchange rates. But in other countries, there are political and currency risks and disclosure isn't as stringent. In Japan, for instance, securities law doesn't require the same degree of information on publicly traded stocks as it does in North America. Despite these problems, there are global technology companies with great merit in other parts of the world, specifically the Far East, Europe, and Israel. Virtually every government in the world wants to create its own version of Silicon Valley. Taiwan is trying to reverse its brain drain by offering its technologically oriented nationals financial incentives to return home. Egypt boasts Pyramid Technology Park and Malaysia has set aside $40 billion and 750 square kilometres (468 square miles) south of Kuala Lumpur to build its own high-tech super corridor.

It is hard for any sensible investor anywhere in the world to consider a technology opportunity without, at the very least, doing a comparison to an American company in the same business. The obvious political differences lead to differences in valuation. To account for the different market dynamics and political risks, investors considering investing in Korea, for instance, would expect to find a lower price to earnings or price to cash flow ratio than if they were buying an American company. "Our approach is to try to find the best core technologies by country and evaluate them for risk profile," says Ian Ainsworth, fund manager for the Altamira Science and Technology Fund.

New technologies are typically launched first in the US where one can assess what the total market might be. It gives the investor an opportunity for a second chance to cash in on a concept that works. If there has been good success in North America, it's fair to surmise that the products will roll out well to other parts of the world. With technology, there are no cultural gaps.

Outside of Canada and the US, huge entrepreneurial growth stories are a lot less common. The European players in technology tend to be huge conglomerates like Sweden's Ericcson, Germany's Siemans, or France's Alcatel. There have been a number of attempts to analyse why Silicon Valley, as well as areas such as Route 128 in Massachusetts, North Austin, and Ottawa's Kanata region, have emerged as centres for the technology industry. The relative flexibility of capital and labour in North America has certainly helped, as has a free-wheeling, entrepreneurial environment and an educational climate that encourages technological research. The proximity of universities with strong engineering and business schools, such as Stanford, University of Texas, Harvard, MIT, and Duke have certainly added to the business environment and provided a ready source of eager talent.

Investing in Technology Around the World

The United States is the most developed in the breadth and diversity of technology companies. The level of understanding of technology businesses and the acceptance of technology as

a specialist investment area is the most mature in the US. About 60 to 65 per cent of the world technology companies are quoted on the US exchanges.

It's only relatively recently on markets around the world that technology has become something which people regard as a worthwhile specialization, and where people specifically look at this sector. Most of the companies outside of the US are young developing companies which are, by definition, small-cap stocks completely new to even the larger institutional investors in the United States. These stocks are difficult to understand unless you live in those markets.

In technology, Canada is at the speculative end of the stock market spectrum. Probably the next most mature technology markets would be in the UK and Scandinavia. The continental European countries in Southern Europe have little in the way of technology-based businesses to invest in. In Germany and France, the supply of technology companies is still relatively limited, and enthusiasm for technology investing tends to be confined to investing in the US market. There is also quite an enthusiasm among most Italian and Swiss investors for the technology sector in the States.

The most interesting technology market in the Far East is in Taiwan. With very high activity and a developing technology industry, it is trying very hard to emulate the US model with the most rapid growth in new companies. The Chinese have an enormous enthusiasm to play the stock market and they gamble prodigiously. In the same way we might walk into a casino, they play the market.

Japan is a funny mishmash of companies. The sector has been in relative decline since the video boom of 1982 and 1983 and Japan is very weak in key technology sectors. While there are a lot of technology-based businesses, they are heavily consumer or industrially based. The Japanese are suffering from competition in much the same way the Europeans and the Americans were challenged by the Japanese 10 to 20 years ago. Their competition is coming from Taiwan and Korea, and eventually it will come from China and India.

Singapore is very enthusiastic about building a technology industry, and to date, that industry is almost entirely built around the disk-drive industry and, to a lesser extent, semiconductor foundries. Ten or 15 years ago, any new emerging economy wanted to build a steel industry, a shipbuilding industry, or an automobile industry. Now countries which desire an economic presence in the world want to be in the technology industry.

Singapore sees itself as a clean, highly computer-literate society. But interestingly, the most successful technology industries tend to emerge from countries with a relatively free thinking and an undisciplined educational structure. Singapore is a tightly disciplined society which doesn't encourage much lateral thinking, which is also true of Korea and Japan. The educational structure in those countries lends itself to technology businesses built on manufacturing rather than on intellectual property.

There is a tremendous amount of technology in Israel spurred by the immigration of Russian scientists, but it is of questionable quality. From an investment standpoint, Israel is quite a tricky market. The propensity for disasters in technology investing in Israel is possibly exceeded only by Vancouver. You need a lot of different ingredients for a successful technology industry, and strong pure research is one of them, something enabled by the defence budget. Obviously a lot of pure technology research and development in Israel has been subsidized by the defence industry, but that's also true of the United States, and of Canada to some degree.

Clearly geographical diversification reduces volatility. The technology industry is growing very rapidly outside of the US where the universe of companies was relatively limited only 10 years ago. There are massive companies being formed in Asia and Europe, and a whole new generation of entrepreneurs is coming along. Eventually, the expansion of technology companies in these markets will make them stronger rivals to the Americans.

Most major technology trends emerge in North America and gradually feed into other countries, but there is a time lag. So if you understand the trends going on in the United States, you have the opportunity to play them over again in the rest of the world and get two or three bites of the cherry. You can take advantage of the networking trend in the US, for example, and then get the opportunity to take advantage of the same trend all over again in Asia and Europe.

Because the brokerage industry is relatively immature outside the US, the quality of research is inconsistent and the incidence of pricing anomalies much greater, the opportunity to exploit proven trends at often unusual prices prevails. Technology spending, as a percentage of global income, has been rising steadily for the last 20 years. In a sophisticated market like Japan, it is at about half the level it is in the US. Over time, these gaps have narrowed and one can be pretty sure global technology spending is going to grow even more significantly. As an investor, you are accessing the fastest-growing segment of the global economy. Ultimately, the earnings growth translates to price performance.

Brian Ashford-Russell,
technology manager, Henderson Investors, London

"I would define technology as anything that changes the way people live and work," says Neil Nisker of Nisker and Associates Strategic Growth Management, which manages individual high-tech portfolios of more than $1 million. "Anything that can change the way people behave is something worth investing in." With so much worth investing in, it is hard to know what to pick. Nisker's central investment premise is based on the principle that it's not how much you make, it's how much you keep from losing. While it is easy enough to pick technology investments that are good, the problem is to not make investments in companies that will hurt the performance of the overall portfolio. "When you consider what industry you could have lost the most money in, it would be technology," he says. "The technology sector has performed very well, but a lot of companies didn't do very well at all."

All technology becomes outdated eventually. Innovation works its way into the market so quickly that corrections happen rapidly. Even the best technology companies in the world, and their spiralling stocks, have to be treated with caution. Who can say for sure when the era of the mainframe, or the word processor, or the router will pass, and the age of something faster, cheaper and better will come along?

DO YOUR HOMEWORK

For $130 dollars, you can buy Bill Gates' brainpower. For me to be able to tap into that man's head for only $130 per share is a great deal. He's the best money manager I know. Why would I want to ask anybody else?

From the Experienced Investor

It's all around you. Read the financial papers and magazines, watch television, talk to your kids, surf the Net, go to a cyber-café, and the buzz is all about technology. Pay attention and you'll find out a lot. If you hang out with people who invest in this sector, you'll hear what they are into. But remember, they usually tell you about their winners and not their losers, and by the time they tell you, chances are it's too late. It harks back to the real estate boom of the early eighties when the cocktail conversation was all about property. Let's hope technology doesn't follow the pattern too closely.

Read Them or Weep

Knowledge and information are the keys to successful investing. By law, the information is there for everyone to look at. Full disclosure is a key requirement of all public stock transactions, meaning that all pertinent data must be provided so that investors can base their decisions on the most complete and accurate information. New companies trading publicly for the first time have to issue a prospectus, while established companies are required to publish an annual report outlining their financial situation. Investors don't need sophisticated legal and accounting training to understand these documents, just a modicum of common sense.

The Prospectus

A prospectus can be the determining factor in the decision of whether or not to buy the securities offered by a new company. The basic requirement of a prospectus is that "full, true, and plain disclosure of all material facts relating to the securities offered" must be made, including all possible pitfalls. Essentially, the prospectus contains a description of the company including its history, operation, assets, officers, and audited financial statements, as well as its future business plans.

There are the various stages as the company prepares to make its shares available to the public.

Draft Prospectus

This is prepared for internal use by the underwriters, the investment dealers issuing the security, and contains fundamental details on the company.

Preliminary Prospectus

This prospectus contains more detail than the draft version, but it can be amended at any time until the final prospectus has been issued. The function of the preliminary prospectus is to gauge the extent of public interest in the issue while it is being reviewed by a securities commission. In the 1920s, investment bankers began calling preliminary prospectuses "red herrings" to warn investors that the documents were not complete or final. The cover of the prospectus was printed in red to identify it as a preliminary document.

Final Prospectus

This is the document that has to contain the full details on the securities being offered for sale. According to US Securities and Exchange Commission (SEC) regulations, the final prospectus must contain details such as management background, aims and goals, the price, distribution spread, use of the proceeds of the issue, and highlights of the securities' attributes.

If you are brave enough to risk investing in an initial public offering (IPO), your stockbroker should provide you with a company prospectus so you can evaluate the warnings. The prospectus will give insight into why a company is issuing shares to raise capital and what the proceeds will be used for.

The Annual Report

In its annual report, an established company has to tell its shareholders, and prospective shareholders how it is doing. There are four financial statements in the annual report:

- Balance sheet

- Profit or loss statement

- Retained earnings statement

- Statement of changes in financial position

The balance sheet gives a snapshot of assets and liabilities and shows a company's financial position at a given point in time. The profit or loss statement shows revenues and expenses for the last year and summarizes activities during the year. The retained earnings statement is the amount that is being reinvested or drawn from the company's balance sheet. The statement of changes in financial position fills in the gaps by providing information about how the operating activities affect the company's cash resources. A review of these changes over a number of years can highlight trends which might otherwise go unnoticed.

The numbers in the financial statements give the investor one impression of the company, its products, and its management. You get another kind of feel by "looking at the pictures," to use the analysts' terminology. The "pictures" are the textual parts of the annual report including the comments and observations of the senior executives, formally called Management's Discussion and Analysis of Financial Conditions and Result of Observations, as well as the photographs. The pictures give management a forum to put its spin on why the numbers came out the way they did and could provide a clue on which parts of the financial statements might warrant special attention.

Don't ignore the footnotes, where a company's corporate secrets might be hidden. These contain such useful information as the company's valuation and depreciation methodology, tax situation, debt structure, dominant customers and suppliers, and foreign exposure.

Ten Signs to Look for in an Annual Report

1. **Is the report forthright?** If it sounds too good to be true, it probably is. An alarm bell should go off if there is all good news and no bad news. Watch for a balanced approach. Truthfulness is very important. If certain items don't add up, be sceptical.

2. **Is it written to be understood?** Simplicity is important. After all, if you can't understand what you are reading, then you can't understand what is being offered.

3. **Does the report convey a sense of the company's goals and values?** There is more to a company than the numbers. How does the company view its employees and the communities it serves?

4. **Does the report include a shareholders' information page?** The amount of dividends paid to shareholders, who the majority owners are, and where to call for information give the reader an indication of how the company is performing.

5. **Is the company's dividend and compensation policy explained?** If not, the prospective shareholder should ask what the policy is and why it is not included in the annual report.

6. **Does the report offer segmented data?** Many larger companies have divisions and subsidiaries. The investor wants to know how all the divisions are doing, how management is dealing with divisions that are dragging down the performance of the company as a whole, and if the company is focusing on the segments with growth potential.

7. **Does the report discuss the competitiveness of the company's product?** This indicates how the product is performing within its market. Companies may present a rosy picture of profits without mentioning that they are losing market share. It may be necessary to find independent data through industry associations or through such independent research companies as the Gartner Group and IDC.

8. **Does the report provide historical information?** Most companies provide up to 10 years of performance data. Of course in the technology sector, many companies haven't been around that long.

9. **Does the report provide an outlook for the future?** A forecast can help the reader understand the direction in which the company sees itself going. Base your judgement on whether the company is continuing to research its market and applying its findings.

10. **Does the report go beyond the legal requirements?** The laws for corporate disclosure are pretty stringent, but as a shareholder, no matter how small, you are one of the owners of the company. You have the right to know how your investment is being managed. The information contained in the annual report should be simple to understand, well-organized, and thorough.

Technology Analysts: A Breed Apart

Analysts hardly ever say sell. The worst term they are likely to utter is "hold," which in analyst lingo actually means sell. What is already factored into a stock's price is expectation. So if a quarterly result is good but not up to expectation, that will be reflected in the analyst's report. But if an objective isn't met when nobody expected the company to meet it anyway, the stock price might not be affected. It is a lot easier if expectations are kept low, so the news you hear from analysts is usually cautious. While the caution has a Chicken Little quality to it, the message is clear: Despite the incredible growth, keep your cool.

Interpreting the Code

Often you'll see analysts reduce a stock to a short-term buy. What does short term mean? Two weeks, two minutes, two hours, two years? Or they'll downgrade from a buy to accumulate. What does accumulate mean? Or they'll cut it from strong buy to buy. I never buy anything with a strong buy. To me it has nowhere to go on the analyst meter but down.

From the Experienced Investor

The first to hear from analysts, not surprisingly, are their best customers — the institutional and professional investors who move millions in and out of the market and profits into the coffers of their investment houses. By the time word filters down to the individual investor, the scenario has probably changed already.

The analysts' opinions are well founded on fact and research. They spend hours at their desks sifting information. Whether you are relying on them or not, it's always a good idea to pay attention. But it is also worthwhile to get a second and a third opinion. It is better to have access to analysts' reports from more than one firm, preferably ones who have not taken the company public. "If you have friends who are investing with Nesbitt Burns and you trade with Midland Walwyn, exchange reports. Sit down over coffee and discuss them" is Robert MacLellan's advice.

These reports are written by specialists who have the contacts and ways of finding out things long before the individual investor can. But in the high-tech sector, there are so many new players in technology analysis that it is hard to know who the best analysts are. In the United States, besides the traditional giant brokerage houses like Merrill Lynch and Goldman Sachs, some specialized investing boutiques have emerged with respected analysis about technology. The opinions of the analysts at Hambrecht & Quist, Robertson Stephens & Company, and Montgomery Securities Inc. on the west coast, and Alex Brown and Sons, Inc. in Baltimore, are highly regarded.

Analysts regularly get to talk to the company principals. Some of the more sophisticated and widely followed companies hold regularly scheduled conference calls or meetings. Since by law all investors are supposedly equal and entitled to the same information, at these private gatherings the CEOs and the CFOs never offer advice or opinion. They give, to use that great Wall Street euphemism, "guidance." If they can, individual investors buying an issue should talk to the inner circle who have met with management and had an opportunity to listen to the story firsthand. "The chairman of AT&T is not going to call you or me first," says Jonathan Steinberg, publisher and editor of *Individual Investor*. "He's going to call the analyst at Merrill Lynch or Goldman Sachs."

Certainly among the first that they call is the San Francisco–based investment bank and brokerage firm Hambrecht & Quist, which specializes in technology. Their senior technology analyst, Doug van Dorsten, thinks a good equity analyst can, with some preparation, do a reasonably good job looking at any sector. However, the technology analyst encounters situations he might not see in other sectors. "I think it's fair to say that technology analysts experience more rapid business cycles and more rapid product cycles than analysts in other sectors," Van Dorsten says.

When they look at technology companies, analysts need a context to understand them. In analysing consumer durables, for instance, it is relatively straightforward to go to the local appliance store and ask questions about refrigerators or ranges to get some idea of the market. Besides the financial evaluation, earnings, growth, and momentum, analysts also look at the technology itself, and decide through their appraisal of the product if the company is a good buy. Having a technical background can give them that context.

The Magic

I'm a scientist and an engineer, and I'm a business person. A good strong basis in physics and mathematics is definitely proper. But you need more than science. You can't put a scientist into the market and say, "Here, figure it out." You have to have somebody with a science background and an MBA, or a good deal of industry experience in this particular sector. Putting all these things together still doesn't make a good analyst. The person may have all the academic qualifications, but not make the grade. Either this person's going to be good at this or he's not. There's an element of magic that you can't identify.

John Drolet, senior technology analyst, Yorkton Securities

Edward Jamieson, portfolio manager for Franklin Resources Inc., doesn't agree that an analyst needs to understand the technology to be effective for his or her clients. His own background is business, finance, and accounting. "The important thing is that you know people who understand technology," he says. "Peter Lynch told a great story about L'Eggs stockings his wife found in the grocery store and liked. Based on the financials, he knew it would be a good investment. He didn't have any more idea about how they make L'Eggs stockings than I do about how they make semiconductors. The fact is that it works and people like and buy it."

Investor Bram Kirshner feels that sometimes the context doesn't give analysts the right perspective for the individual investor. "They see their role as trying to understand the technology, to look five or 10 years down the road to find the next Microsoft. They feel that anybody can say, 'Gee, it's cheap, let's buy it.' They don't look at evaluation, they look at the technology for 20 years hence." But not every analyst is brash enough to claim an insider's track to all the knowledge. "Our crystal ball is as cloudy as the next guy's," says Chip Morris, manager of the T. Rowe Price Science and Technology Fund, the leading American technology fund. Analysts like to look at earnings. But, as we have already gathered, earnings aren't always the best measure for technology stocks. Sometimes by looking at other measures, you can invest against the consensus of the analysts. What you want to look for is someone who thinks differently, who thinks outside the box.

One Analyst's Strategy

As the largest investment house in Canada, RBC Dominion Securities Inc. has an enormous variety of clients with a range of investing styles. Some have an appetite for an aggressive growth portfolio. Others have a more conservative inclination. Benn Mikula, RBC Dominion's director of research, was ranked top technology analyst in the Brendan Wood International consulting firm's annual survey of analysts. He outlines his firm's approach to staying on top.

"In our research, we highlight the relative risk parameters. For instance, Newbridge Network Corp., a long-time recommendation of the firm, has done a wonderful job sustaining shareholder value, but we remind our clients it trades in a volatile fashion, though with a strong upward bent. No question Newbridge with $1.4 billion in revenue and thousands of employees

is a big, well-established blue chip company, but probably causes a few more heart beats than a utility company."

By focusing on specialized sectors of technology with one
analyst for networking and telecommunications equipment,
another for semiconductors, and another for enterprise software,
RBC can make an assessment about the merits, health, and
growth prospects of the subsector as a whole. They can evaluate
the relative balance between companies and how technological
shift and product and pricing developments may affect the group.

What Are the Chances?

Even the most brilliant analyst is only going to have about a 65
per cent success rate. So if you ask him on any given day what
his favourite stock is, he has about a one in three chance of giving you a dog.

Rob Millham, manager of research, C.M. Oliver and Company

The Underwriting Effect

Underwriting is the process whereby investment bankers, or
underwriters, buy a new issue of securities from a company and
resell them to the public. The details of the underwriter's agreement includes the underwriter's promise to purchase the issue; the
issue's public offering price, the underwriting spread, the settle-
ment date, and the issuer's net proceeds. Watching underwriters is
an especially interesting way to find new companies coming to
market. Some underwriters are more tapped in than others. Some
have reputations for discovering new technology opportunities
and that reputation can rub off on an emerging company, can give
the investor more confidence, and can influence the price.

Goldman Sachs, Morgan Stanley, Robertson Stephens, Hambrecht & Quist, Montgomery Securities, and Alex Brown and Sons are among the most well-connected investment houses likely to be underwriting the better-performing technology companies. Investors can investigate whether these brokers are involved in the offering transaction to determine its viability.

Choosing a Broker: Full-Service or Discount?

Full-Service Brokers

Choosing a broker is a critical step for any first-time investor. When you choose a full-service broker, you are picking somebody to give you advice and guidance, so it's got to be somebody you trust. The brokerage house typically has a research department — the analysts we have been talking about. Full-service brokers will use their knowledge to make recommendations on buying, selling, and holding securities. That research isn't free. It is factored into the sizeable commissions these full-service brokers charge for completing a transaction.

"It's very hard for one person, even one professional, to manage a portfolio of technology stocks without either a professional manager or a broker who is very well tied into technology analysts," Franklin Resources money manager Edward Jamieson says. "That person has to rely on other people's knowledge and leverage their ideas."

Whether you win or lose, the broker charges you a commission, so, although securities rules say that the broker has to get to know the client, it is even more important for the client to get to know the broker. The best way to find a broker is through referral, but don't go with the first recommendation. Shop around until you find the one who is right for you. Make a list of questions to ask each candidate in your initial meeting. (See the following "Checklist" for ideas.)

While you are hoping that the broker will help you make money, your broker is assured to make money from you. It's your money and your call, and you can easily take your business down the street.

Checklist for Choosing a Broker

Qualifications: Does the potential broker have the proper education to follow technology stocks, and is he or she keeping up with refresher courses?

Experience: How many years of experience does the broker have as an advisor, and what degree of expertise and what percentage of time is spent practising in the technology sector?

Specialization: Does the broker understand technology issues?

Compatible personality: Does the broker display the communication skills, attitude, approach, candour, and commitment to meet your needs?

Objectivity: Is the advice you get tainted in any way by bias or personal financial benefit?

Trust: Do you intuitively trust the advice as being solely in your best interests?

Comparison: What can this broker offer that the one down the street can't?

If you do decide to use a full-service broker don't be afraid to negotiate the commission. The broker is likely to tell you that the commission rate is set by the investment house, but the truth of the matter is that the more you trade the more likely it is that you can get a break on the price. You can be sure that the institutional investors aren't paying anywhere near as much as the retail investors. If you are paying six per cent, on each transaction, a not unheard of sum, it means your stock has to appreciate by 12 per cent for you to break even.

Discount Brokers

Since you are reading this book, you probably have a certain amount of investing sophistication, and since you are interested in investing in this sector, it is likely that you have a tolerance for risk and confidence in your own stock-picking abilities. You might be the ideal customer for a discount brokerage firm, the investment industry's equivalent of the no-frills airline. Don't expect investment advice, research, or hand-holding. It is strictly a transactional procedure, the mechanical execution of a trade without comment or intervention. And with telephone and Internet trading, you can't even expect a flesh-and-blood person at the other end of the transaction. It's strictly do-it-yourself, but as a result, you don't pay the hefty commissions and fees charged by full-service brokers.

There are many other sources of information besides analysts' reports, and these are outlined later in this chapter. Furthermore, investing in technology stocks is so new that you might discover that you have more expertise than the broker who wants to handle your account. With so much activity and so many players in the market, managing a portfolio of technology stocks is challenging. The best approach is probably to use both a discount broker and a full-service broker. But be fair. If you are influenced by a broker's advice and research, acknowledge it by trading with that firm and paying the price. You will probably be rewarded with further good investing ideas. However, if you did it all on your own, why share the reward?

Good News, Bad News

There are degrees of bad news. You'll hear: "The company is going to underperform this quarter. They're going to be two pennies below the consensus estimate." The consensus estimate is simply the average appraisal of all the analysts following the stock. Estimates are a fool's game because, lo and behold, most firms manage to beat the estimates. If the firm underperforms, first you have to understand why. Is it an anomaly that will last a quarter or two, and create fresh buying opportunities? Or is it the beginning of something nasty: the product doesn't work, the trials are coming back bad, there's been a recall, the competition is killing them, or similar really bad news.

When to Take the Chance

You have to be particularly careful about whether business fundamentals are deteriorating. Some companies have a one- or two-quarter product problem. For instance, their customers might be aware that a new product is coming and stop ordering the old one. If you know the company's franchise is still intact and new products are actually shipping (and by the way, you've seen a favourable review in *PC Magazine*), the management's great, and they've always had high profit margins in the past, then you can count on the company snapping out of it. If you have an 80 per cent confidence level that this is only a one-quarter glitch, go ahead and buy into the panic.

Paul Wick, manager,
Seligman Communications and Information Fund

Good news should have an immediate dollar value attached to it. If you hear good news but you don't see sales contracts being signed, and if you don't hear favourable analyst reports, begin to get nervous. If good news doesn't translate into sales, as an investor you should be trying to get the meaning from the message. "Talented PR and investor relations people do a very good job telling you the product is the greatest thing since the

invention of the bagel," Robert MacLellan, an analyst with Warburg Dillon Read, says. "Then you see it at a trade show and you
say 'you've got to be kidding me.' If it doesn't look as if contracts
are coming, then its strictly good PR."

These fantastic claims don't mean that the people involved
are unscrupulous. It is often the case of an overabundance of
enthusiasm translating into unrealistic expectations. With newspapers, magazines, TV and radio programs, on-line services, and
scuttlebutt, sources of information are plentiful. Investors can
find out quite a lot if they put their mind to it. No matter what
the source, though, you have to read it critically and sceptically.
Good journalists never rely on any information unless they can
verify it with another independent source. Investors should be
the same way. After all, it's your money at stake.

In the absence of other information, the last information you
want to read is what the company says, because that's PR.

Robert Ferchat, CEO, BCE Mobile Communications Inc.

Qualitative and Quantitative

There are two types of news — qualitative and quantitative.
Quantitative has to do with the numbers — earnings, revenues,
and profits. Every day, the newspapers report this quantitative
information with quotes from analysts and experts. For the short
term, this quantitative information affects the performance of
the stock intensely. "I've noticed on NASDAQ if you miss your
earnings, whether it's by a cent or by 20 cents, your stock drops
$5. It's not even on a percentage basis. It's almost a rule," says
venture capitalist Loudon Owen. "If quantitative news is not

managed well, you see that precipitous $5 drop." During report-
ing season, every analyst looks at the results and the company
commentary and makes an assessment as to whether that's consistent with the forecasts. Technology is so driven by momentum, that even if the reports are off by a penny, even if it is only
for one quarter, the forecast can change dramatically.

But as we have already discussed, the information about technology stocks that matters is qualitative, and that is subjective,
making it notoriously difficult to understand and dissect. "We do
lots of number crunching to evaluate a company," says Doug van
Dorsten, senior technology analyst for Hambrecht & Quist. "But
products drive sales and sales drive everything else, including
profit margins. So to assess the potential for continuing success,
you have to assess the products. This qualitative assessment of the
products happens at the front end of all your quantitative work."

Rick Serafini doesn't just use a slide rule to pick the companies for the Trimark Discovery Fund. He also uses a qualitative
approach. The approach focuses on: first, the company's business
model; second, the key people who will execute the critical
functions; and third, the forward, or growth, opportunities. "The
basic building blocks of design, sales, marketing, administration,
and operations don't deviate that much from sector to sector or
industry to industry," he says. "My approach is to understand
each of those building blocks and what economic value they
should produce."

Between the Lines

You learn to read between the lines when you read a technology
company prospectus or annual report. Common sense and
healthy scepticism, not cynicism, about a company's excessive
optimism can help you cut through the blather to the bone. The
annual report and the annual general meeting gives the investor

a first-hand opportunity to size up management and to get a tone of their overall philosophies and methodologies. The annual report tells you how innovative the company is in its management style. It contains all kinds of important facts, such as what incentives are being used to retain key employees, and how much is being spent on research and development.

Listen Up

If you read speeches of CEOs, like any good politicians, they're probably not telling you the exact truth. If you're reading financial information of a careful disclosure, watch what they don't say, particularly for American listed companies, where they can be sued. If the wording is too precise, think about what they've excluded from the wording. You have to look out for the nuances.

Robert Ferchat, CEO, BCE Mobile Communications Inc.

"The annual meeting is the one time in the year when management has to stand before its shareholders and the investing community and say, 'Gee whiz, we've done a great job and, oh, by the way, here's where we see ourselves moving forward,'" says Royal Bank investment manager Robert McWhirter who, as the largest technology investor in Canada, has attended many annual meetings and read countless reports.

Even Ted Carter, a trader prepared to take a risk for a fat return, is cautious. Like any good investor he wants to be informed before he stakes his money. He finds that he's often baffled when he tries to understand a technology company report because he doesn't have technical expertise. Instead, he watches the market dynamics to determine the viability of a stock. As he puts it:

"If I contact the people involved with a mining company, I can understand what the heck they're talking about. With most of the high-tech companies, I don't. So I just go along and say, 'Hey, this looks like pretty good news to me, and does the market think the same way.' I don't even know what somebody would pay for a new technology product. But for a mining company with a discovery and no earnings, I know what somebody would pay for the gold in the ground."

Bad news can sometimes be good news for the well-informed investor. Remember that the stock market doesn't reflect what a security is actually worth, only what others think it is worth. Bad news in the financial press can trigger a stampede away from a stock that still has good value. A sell recommendation from a high-profile analyst can provoke a dramatic cycle of sell-offs. The sell-off pressure might leave a bargain in its wake and create an opportunity to buy.

It's a cliché that once you hear about a stock everybody else has heard about it already. The accepted hypothesis of an efficient market says the price of a stock has already been discounted to reflect the news. The truth is that the exchange of information can be so rapid these days that the professionals and insiders don't have that much lead time any more. In fact, there are so many sources of information and the market moves so rapidly that if you do not work in investments full time it is tough to keep up. The advantage the pros have is that they are watching the market all the time. Though technology is narrowing the gap, professionals have the time, resources, and the tools to balance all this information in their decision making.

Bram Kirshner feels that we already live in an age when information is instantaneous and this, he believes, has levelled the playing field. "Ten years ago, it would have been very hard for a small investor like me to find out everything I needed to know about a company. Now, through the Internet, and through very inexpensive services, I can find out everything I need to know about a stock in a matter of minutes."

Taking It to the Streets

Technology is all about trends. The Peter Lynch school of investing tells us to look around and see what companies you like which seem to be popular. Peter Lynch, who managed the Fidelity Magellan Fund and wrote *One Up on Wall Street*, was talking about consumer goods and retailing. These days the trends are in technology, where jobs are being created in the technology field. Everybody has a friend who works with computers. Talk to them. Or wander into the back office at your place of business and find what their plans are for computing, networking, and telecommunications. Richard Woo, the high-tech analyst at Thomson Kernaghan & Co., suggests visiting a few electronic stores and asking the salespeople which computers are selling. "Check out which companies are offering discounts, because sales usually indicate a build-up of inventory. If prices are dropping, you know that there is more supply than demand."

Even if the news has already been discounted, it's not too late to follow trends. Following the news gives you a chance to guess the next move, not analyse the last one. For example, an acquisition has probably already been anticipated in the market. But now that you know the company's strategy is acquisition, you can determine if it will make another one.

A Resource Guide

The $50 or so that you spend on a newspaper or magazine subscription could save you or make you a lot of money.

Robert MacLellan, analyst, Warburg Dillon Read

Knowledge is power. Investors are always looking for the secret formula for picking stocks. They listen to "hot" tips from their brother-
in-law, their taxi driver, someone on the bus, or they follow
"educated" tips from experts on television, in newspapers, or in
newsletters. These tips are useful clues because they give you a starting point to investigate further. Before you buy a car, at the very least
you start the engine and kick the tires. You read *Consumer Reports* or
Car and Driver and ask your mechanic for his opinion. It might seem
obvious, but why wouldn't you subject a stock to the same scrutiny?

Free information about stocks is available from brokerages,
public relations firms, and the investor relations departments of the
companies themselves. The more attention a company can generate, the more interest investors will have in following its fortune
and the bigger the pool of potential investors will be. By law, public companies are required to send out quarterly and annual reports
no matter how good or bad the news is. Every shareholder is entitled to know exactly what is happening to his or her investment and
legally the company cannot hide the facts, unpleasant as they might
be. While it is illegal for a company to intentionally — or uninten-
tionally — distort facts or mislead the shareholders, annual and
quarterly reports are carefully written by expert communicators to
put a positive spin on the company story. As we explained earlier in
this chapter, it is not that hard to decipher the code in an annual
report, but the nuances must be weighed carefully.

The investor relations department of any company is glad to
forward a copy of the annual report to potential investors. Many
companies now post their annual reports automatically on the
Internet. More complete annual reports (10K) and quarterly
reports (10Q) are filed with the Securities and Exchange Commission in the United States and with the provincial securities
commissions in Canada. Financial newspapers and magazines
will forward selected annual reports to their readers on request.
Some investors check off all the technology and biotechnology
companies on the request list and wait for the mail delivery.

Most people still get their information from the financial newspapers — the *Wall Street Journal* and *Investors Business Daily* in the United States and the *Globe and Mail's Report on Business* and the *Financial Post* in Canada. The *Financial Times* of London offers a more international perspective on investing. In the United States, radio and television cater to the growing appetite for business news. CNBC, CNNfn, Bloomberg TV, *The Nightly Business News Report*, and *Wall Street Week* with Louis Rukeyser are around-the-clock sources of information, at least while the North American markets are open. In Canada, there is less investment information in the mass media, but the supply is growing to meet the demand with the *Globe and Mail's* proposed all-business specialty channel, the recent upgrading of investment information on CBC News-world's expanded *Newsworld Business News*, and a report every quarter hour on CTV's headline news service, *CTV News 1*.

Business newsmagazines and periodicals are focusing more and more on investing in technology with *Business Week, Forbes, Fortune, Money, Smart Money, Individual Investor* and *Worth* gracing almost every newsstand. "*Smart Money* is the best magazine," says one technology investor. "It's user-friendly and everything a business magazine should be. *Business Week* is like *Time* magazine. By the time I read it, I know all about it, it's old news, or it really doesn't relate to my needs."

The Red Herring and *Upside* are magazines designed specifically for the technology investor and they offer perceptive insight into the business of the industry. *Red Herring*, also available on the Internet at www.herring.com, describes itself as a provider of business information for the technology industry, giving readers an inside look at the latest deals and strategies, and the latest rumblings in the world of strategic finance, from the trading floor to the boardroom. *Upside*, www.upside.com, calls itself the business magazine for the technology elite, with an insider's view of the world's leading technology companies.

The Internet seems almost created for information about technology investment. Entering "technology" and "investing" into the AltaVista search engine gives you over 37,000 returns. Every publicly traded company has its own site that contains relevant information about its products and stock pricing, including, in some cases, analysts' reports. Every investment house, money manager, and financial advisor has an address on the Web. All the financial media also publish on the Web, some with a fee and some for free. Chat groups about investing abound and many of them concentrate on technology companies. Of course, as with any information, look to the messenger to be sure there is no vested interest. The drawback with chat groups is that you don't know who you're listening to, or whether the information is biased. You can't tell if somebody in the group is touting a particular stock because they love it, or if they are trying to drum the price up to get out, or if they are short sellers looking to create rumours. On-line, you can get honest, bona fide mom-and-pop investors talking to professionals using a pseudonym. Take what you see on the chat lines with a big grain of salt.

Having said that, particularly popular sites for investors in technology are The Motley Fool, www.fool.com, and Silicon Investor, www.techstocks.com. Needless to say, they aren't everybody's favourites. "I have really mixed feelings because forums like Motley Fool can be easily manipulated," says Doug van Dorsten, senior technology analyst with Hambrecht & Quist. "I think it's a wonderful source for on-line public information of a company, but I also think it's very dangerous for people to depend wholly on someone they don't know."

Five Steps to Safe Surfing

1. **Be Your Own Watchdog**. Remember the Internet is unregulated. Anything goes.

2. **Question All Advice**. Since you don't know the source of information or the motives behind them, challenge the validity of anything you read.

3. **Measure Twice and Cut Once**. Always get a second opinion.

4. **Do Your Homework**. Diligence is always better than disappointment.

5. **Use Good Judgement**. If something seems too good to be true, chances are it is.

Because of all the information available, the investing playing field has evened out. The individual investor is still not at par with the institutional investor, but the balance is much closer. Daily, especially in the United States, individual investors get the best and brightest minds of Wall Street visiting their homes via television and other media. The challenge is to sift through this volume of information and often contradictory opinion.

In theory, news is made available to everybody at the same time. The news is disseminated to analysts, portfolio managers, and news services without delay. They tell stockbrokers, and at once it is relayed to individual investors and to on-line services. With the ready availability of information in this day and age of the Internet and on-line access to brokerage reports, the individual investor should be able to make very informed judgements.

There is nothing like doing your homework. If you're going to invest hard-earned money, it's worth the time to study not only the market but also the industry and the company. Too many investors go on very little information — a single article in the newspaper or a couple of conversations. Given the Internet, the World Wide Web, 10Qs, 10Ks, and the like, it's worth taking the time to review the kinds of things the company is involved in and where it is going, as we shall see in the next chapter.

WHAT TO BUY: THE RECIPE FOR SUCCESS

Buy It on Sale

As an individual, I tend to buy stocks that are relatively inexpensive, or inexpensive relative to the growth potential. I look for stories that are out of favour and companies that have had some product problems which appear to be improving. If a particular company is selling for one times revenue and maybe 10 or 15 times earnings, I like it. I like to buy cheap stock. It's my nature.

Douglas van Dorsten,
senior technology analyst, Hambrecht & Quist

There is no question that everybody should hold technology in their portfolios. The question is, how much. One way to calculate it might be to use economic sector diversification — diversify your portfolio in proportion to the distribution of sectors in the economy. In the United States, you might use the Standard & Poor's 500 Index as an indicator. The stocks on the S&P 500 are selected because they reflect the economy, and right now, 15.5 per cent of this composite index portfolio is in technology. In Canada, the TSE 300 Index currently has about 7.5 per cent of its holdings in technology and biotechnology stocks. And that proportion is going up very fast.

Another indicator investors might use to weight their portfolios is percentage of gross domestic product. Technology is climbing towards 30 per cent of GDP, and the technology research companies are forecasting growth at 15 per cent per year. In the semiconductors subsector, growth is projected at closer to 19 per cent. At this rate, inside an economy that's growing at between 3 and 4 per cent, within five years, technology will no longer be a sliver in the stock market. Another way to measure is to check what professional investors are doing. Currently in the US, the average weighting of technology in a balanced mutual fund stands at 20 per cent.

Stocks are definitely most enticing when they are cheap, and the potential reward is disproportionately greater than the risk. That is not to say that a technology company that appears to be fully valued is a bad buy. Valuations that might seem ridiculously high may be reasonable if you bear in mind that stock values in this sector are based on future results. All things being equal, even if you get a return at the average rate for the stock market, you can expect to be 8 to 10 per cent richer a year from now. The trick is to catch trends that will last and not short-term fads.

The stock market is full of theories and strategies to identify trends and circumstances that are going to influence a stock performance. Some of it is technical number crunching, and some of it is trend spotting. The prediction last year, for instance, was that multimedia was going to drive the technology sector with the advent of DVD, digital video disk, and MMX. We're still waiting. The word for next year is that the time has come for small-capitalization stocks since they have been lagging the big stocks. The forecast is that companies in the Russell 2000 small-cap index — the principal index for small-cap stocks, established by the Frank Russell Company — will see a significant gain. The largest company in the small-cap index has a capitalization of $1.1 billion and the smallest is capitalized at $160 million.

Technology stocks, though highly volatile, will always be market leaders over the long term. Technology stocks have risen nearly three times as fast as the overall market in the 1990s, and it is not unreasonable to think that the rally will continue for years. The bell-wether Pacific Stock Exchange Tech 100 Index has risen 129 per cent since the boom began in June 1994 and has consistently beaten the S&P 500 Index ever since.

But the hallmark of the high-tech industry is sudden swings in company fortunes, with gyrations and corrections in the stocks or even the entire sector. Even the fastest-growing companies are subject to the most merciless trouncing at the first sign of bad news. There's lots of advice for how to ride the wave without crashing to the ground with a thud: "Stick with companies that are relatively early in their product life cycle," says Jim Broadfoot, chief investment officer for Mackenzie Investment Management Inc. in Boca Raton, Florida and co-manager of the Mackenzie Universal World Science and Technology Fund. "But be careful of companies that are going through a product transition."

"Go for companies with big market opportunities and stay away from companies that have slow growth or stagnant markets," says Paul Wick, manager of the Seligman Communications and Information Fund, the best-performing technology fund over the past 10 years. "You'll obviously do well with technology stocks with rising profit margins, especially rising gross profit margins. We definitely like companies with the potential to continue to show very fast top-line growth."

What these and other experts are telling you is very basic. Look for companies that are doing well and that you believe will continue to do well. The best advice is usually the simplest. "It's not brain surgery and we are not brain surgeons," says *Individual Investor* publisher Jonathan Steinberg.

I learned a long time ago that I'm not nearly smart enough to figure out what technology is going to work in the market place. I try
not try to guess when the product will be accepted. I buy it once
it has already been accepted and then I watch the momentum.

Robert Millham, manager of research,
C.M. Oliver & Company Limited

Last year, businesses spent $212 billion on computers and
communication hardware as well as tens of billions of dollars on
software and systems development. Investment in technology
goes up by 24 per cent a year, accounting for almost one-third of
all economic growth. In contrast, spending on industrial
machinery is less than $130 billion. Focusing on companies that
sell to corporations tempers risk with stability. Corporations
have an installed base of technology that they build on, unlike
consumers who are fickle and quick to change when it comes to
their technology. If a company is investing millions of dollars on
systems and applications, it doesn't react to the hype of a new
technology just because it's hot. The chief information officer at
a corporation is betting his job every time he makes a decision
on a new technology. Rest assured he isn't going to jump into
anything before it has been proven it will work in critical circumstances. But once he is committed, he is going to plunge in
with a sizeable order. And if he is staking his job on his decision,
he's more than likely to buy from established companies with a
reputation and with other large customers.

Another way to tame the risk of the technology sector is to
invest in telephone-equipment providers. In the developed world,
deregulation and technological change are transforming the
phone industry from sleepy utility businesses into a high-growth

competitive free-for-all. They are all solid, reliable companies that are growing ever larger, and the right ones are scoring for their investors.

Within the telecommunications subsector, the makers of wireless-phone equipment are a particularly attractive investment. Even more feverish growth in this sub-sector is expected as new technologies, like digital personal communications systems (PCS), roll out and opportunities blossom in the developing world. Exports account for 60 per cent of the revenues of the most successful technology companies, and they are counting on exports as the engines to keep them flourishing.

Many developing regions don't have a modern wire-based telephone infrastructure, and wireless systems can be installed with relative ease. This international opportunity has driven earnings for the world's cellular powers — America's Motorola, Finland's Nokia, Canada's Northern Telecom, and Sweden's Ericsson. They have been growing at 35 to 45 per cent a year, and analysts foresee, conservatively, 15 to 20 per cent annual gains for the next decade. But beware. Sales depend on a growth in these developing economies and they grow by fits and starts. When Motorola announced a shortfall in its revenue expectations because its international sales, especially to China and Eastern Europe, lagged, its stock price dropped drastically, bringing down the rest of its sector before it recovered.

No strategy about what to buy is foolproof because it is all based on conjecture. Just like any other aspect of investing in technology, the best advice is to do your homework and feel comfortable with the relative risk of what you've bought. The hottest tip you can get is to have been in the technology market last year, and almost as good is the advice to be there tomorrow. For the wise investor, technology is the place to be.

Running Hot and Cold

There are so-called hot companies in the market place and so-called cold companies. Hot companies usually are driven by the same excellence — a commonly shared vision and a well-positioned management team. If you find that in a young technology company, then it has a fighting chance of being able to meet or even exceed the market's growth expectations.

Loudon Owen, venture capitalist, McLean Watson Capital Inc.

Playing by the Numbers

You will often hear novice investors moaning about not being able to afford Microsoft or IBM because the stock price is so high. Shrewder investors check the price to earnings ratio to evaluate the true price of a stock. The price to earnings ratio — the P/E or the multiple — is the current market price divided by earnings per share. When Hewlett-Packard was trading at $64 a share and earnings per share were $2.20, its P/E ratio was 29. Meanwhile, IBM was trading at $102 and had earnings per share of $10.24 and its P/E ratio was 9. So at that particular time, though its share price was higher, all other things being equal, IBM would have been a better buy. Though P/E ratio is best used in conjunction with other measures, if two companies of equal stature in the same industry with similar prospects have different P/E ratios, the one with the lower ratio is usually the better buy. If one is earning a million dollars and the other $10 million with the same number of shares, then theoretically, the company earning 10 times as much in sales should be trading at 10 times the price. The average P/E ratio for technology companies is 17.

At the same time the P/E ratio tells you the true value of the stock, it tells you how much confidence investors have in the company. A high multiple says a stock is overvalued; however, it also indicates that investors like its potential. The P/E ratio is an expression of market sentiment toward a company and its stock, so if you track a company's P/E over time you get an indication of how the public response to the company might be changing.

Recent studies of market performance have found that low P/E stocks generally perform better than high P/E stocks. The studies concluded that a stock with a high P/E ratio is already discounted for future growth. Conventional wisdom has it that a P/E ratio of 15 is optimal, meaning the stock is priced correctly or fully valued. Investors looking for a bargain shop with low P/E ratios in mind. However, since small-cap technology stocks don't have much in the way of earnings, it is hard to calculate a multiple, and the P/E of a fully valued technology stock is higher because greater growth is expected. Also, confidence is generally so high in the technology sector that multiples, when they can be be calculated, are way out of proportion to the rest of the market. So in the technology sector, investors have to rethink what constitutes the right price.

The question comes down to how much of a premium investors are prepared to pay for growth and potential. If two companies have the same evaluation but one was growing twice as fast, what is a fair price the investors should pay for that extra growth? Bear in mind that high-growth stocks can turn out to be poor investments when the market has already overpaid for that potential growth. For a growth stock to perform well, it has to exceed the market's expectations. For instance, the market might expect a fast-growing company to grow at 40 per cent, a phenomenal rate in most other sectors. But if it only does that well, the stock price will not rise. The market already expected that growth and will pay the premium only if it exceeds the expectation.

Though price to earnings is the most accepted and widely used ratio, investors are always looking for the magic number that will point to the best buy. Price to cash flow, price to sales, price to earnings growth rate, and price to cash are other ratios that are used. Believe it or not, some serious investors think that the ratio of sales to the number of PhDs within a firm is an indication of its potential success! In a sector as volatile as technology, quantitative measures like ratios are probably best considered along with the qualitative measures that reflect concept, management, and marketing.

There are now stock screening tools on the Internet that allow investors to sift through the data that is available for publicly traded companies. Investors can enter the criteria they think will affect the price of the stock and cross-reference them. Then only those companies that meet the criteria will be selected. These screening tools used to be expensive and available only to elite and institutional investors. With the advent of the Internet, individual investors can get this service virtually free. Sites with screening filters include Hoover Online's StockScreener at www.stockscreener.com, *Research Magazine*'s www.researchmag.com, www.stocktools.com, www.marketguide.com, www.-marketplayer.com, and many others.

The market is going to pay lower multiples on a basic industry stock that's fairly boring than on something that's got a sexy, high-technology story to it. I look at what the markets are willing to pay for similar technology. In the fast-paced networking world, for instance, multiples are going to be high.

Robert Millham, manager of research,
C. M. Oliver & Company Limited

The Psychology of Splits

Those novice investors who moan about the high price of Microsoft and IBM stock are not alone. Even though you get the same return if you buy one share of Microsoft at $135 and it goes up 5 per cent, as you would if you bought 100 shares of Interleaf at $1.35 and it goes up 5 per cent, psychologically, investors feel more comfortable buying shares within a certain absolute price range. Therefore, a company will implement a split if it thinks it can attract more investor demand.

Because investors who see stocks trading at a high absolute price think of it as expensive — like Microsoft at $135, Dell at $123, or IBM at $102 — the company might decide to split the stock so that its absolute price looks more reasonable. For instance, a share that was worth $100 might split two for one, with each of the new shares now worth $50, and an investor who owned 100 shares would now own 200 shares.

Investors like splits because it shows that management has confidence that the market favours the stock. Often a stock that is already showing a lot of momentum and has moved well above its price will split. When a split is announced, momentum in a stock's price continues. Sometimes on the day of the split, a stock price will fall, creating a buying opportunity. But studies have shown that a stock that splits will outperform the market over the next 12 months.

If the price of a stock has been dropping, there might be a consolidation, which is the opposite of a split, so that the absolute price falls within the psychologically acceptable range. In the same way that investors are wary of high absolute prices, they are also frightened by low prices. The best psychological price range is a reflection of how the stock has performed in the past, the stage in the company's development, and how the rest of the market is doing. Studies have shown that investors are most comfortable between $1 and $30, but each investor must find his or her own comfort level. The shares of an established blue-chip company with a high absolute price are usually more attractive than those of a high-priced start-up.

Financial Analysis Made Easy

Since technology companies typically plough their earnings back into their operations, they ordinarily don't pay dividends, so dividend yield isn't a useful measure of value. As you will see, technology companies don't take on a lot of debt, so analysing things such as debt to equity or debt to total capital ratios doesn't make any sense. When they go public, most technology companies are already self-funding and generate positive cash flow with virtually no debt from the start. Because it's not necessary to build large, expensive plants, the requirement for hard assets and access to bank financing to acquire hard assets is also not relevant.

What is always good to measure, no matter what the sector, is the money coming in — cash flow, or revenues. Although stock charts in the business papers always have a column for price to earnings ratio, and it is the first thing investors look at to determine the value of a stock, since many technology companies don't start out with earnings or profits, just potential, technology analysts and investors who talk about price to earnings ratio in this sector really mean price to cash flow ratio.

Investors are always looking for an edge in the way they evaluate the worth of a company. With so many factors to consider, they want to get at the real truth by number crunching, or doing the appropriate financial analysis. Because of the nature of the way technology companies do business, analysts can't use their customary broad-based financial analysis systems.

The Dupont Analysis

One financial analysis technique is the Dupont Analysis. Some of the more technically oriented analysts employ this formula to project what the return on investment will be. Although it is still not mainstream, the Dupont Analysis is gaining currency because the variable factors are readily plotted on a spreadsheet and can be easily manipulated on a computer by the technologically aware. Although the Dupont Analysis is applicable in most industries, technology differs from traditional investing. Still, a basic grasp of the system can show how to analyse a potential investment.

Here comes the number crunching and terminology, which is not all that complicated. Generally, return on investment comes about through two components — the ability to control costs, and the ability to use assets to generate sales. Sales leverage or asset utilization is the term used to refer to the amount of sales generated per dollar of assets. Profit margin is measured by the ability to control costs and the amount of income per dollar of sales. Additional risk is measured by the degree of financial leverage brought about by the use of borrowed funds.

So by calculating the amount of operating income generated per dollar of assets, or the return on investment, the investor can assess whether it is a good business to be in. The amount of net income made available to shareholders per dollar of investment — return on equity — measures the ability of the enterprise to increase the wealth of the owners. The Dupont Analysis considers return on equity to be the most pertinent measure for companies.

For a traditional industrial company, net profit margin even as low as 5 per cent can be considered fairly reasonable. Because it takes a lot of assets to produce a dollar in revenue, asset utilization for a steel mill or a utility company, for example, would be pretty high. And since historically companies use someone else's money — borrowed money or debt — to get a good return on invested capital, leverage can be high as well.

When you apply the head-spinning Dupont Analysis to technology, and software companies in particular, you notice how striking the differences are. Profit margins in this sector are comparatively high, for the best-known software companies typically in the 50 to 80 per cent range. Also, technology companies don't require a lot of fixed assets to produce dollar sales. Their assets are people and leased space, rather than costly raw materials, expensive plants, and machinery.

The preferred method technology companies choose for raising capital is through the equity markets since banks, and other lending institutions, have always been reluctant to lend to companies without fixed assets they can repossess. The demand for equity in technology companies has been so steady that it is rare for them to take on a lot of debt, even when they get the opportunity.

In the technology business, it's hard not to have good asset utilization since the cost to manufacture the product is very low. There's no inventory shrinkage to speak of since these companies don't keep much inventory on hand because their products become obsolete so quickly and unexpectedly. What analysts look for in this sector is the potential for achieving high profit margins, which is a direct function of how popular the product is rather than cost control.

Mergers and Acquisitions

In an industry of sharks and minnows, the bigger fish eat the little fish, which eat the littler fish. In the high-tech industry, takeovers are commonplace and generally amicable. They take place when a company wants to acquire new technologies or distribution channels without going to the trouble of inventing them on its own. An acquisition usually has little to do with the assets or the true market value of a company since the assets of most technology companies are the intellectual capabilities of the principals. So, for an acquisition to be successful, the acquirer has to ensure that the key personnel at the acquired company want to stick around. The top people need an incentive not only to stay with the company, but to perform at their best. For a merger to work, the corporate culture and business practices of both parties must fit strategically. A good fit at the right price can offer real momentum to a business and superb value to the investor. On the other hand, if the investment community thinks a merger isn't working it can hurt the price of the stock. After 3COM Corporation bought U.S. Robotics Corporation in the largest merger in the history of the networking industry, 3COM's share price fell as analysts considered whether the two very different companies could work well together.

An investor who can gauge when the time is ripe for a company to be acquired can reap a bumper return. In the high-tech sector, an acquisition is likely to happen when a stock falls from its highest price, but the price paid in the acquisition will probably be at or beyond that historic high. In the resource industry, another sector rife with acquisitions, takeovers occur when the stock price reaches its highest point, and the price the acquiring company pays goes beyond that historic high price.

Some of the biggest deals ever have come in the technology sector. In the past four years, Microsoft has spent more than $2.5 billion on 57 acquisitions, partnerships, and joint ventures. It's the way Microsoft became the behemoth it is and the strategy Cisco used to grow so quickly and powerfully. Their competitors have followed their example. Telecommunications is also consumed with mergers and divestitures, but very seldom are these cash deals. The acquirer usually offers its own stock to pay the price of an acquisition. Technology companies' incredible cash flow allows them to buy back their stock. Then, when the right opportunity arises, they use that stock, which has usually inflated in value, to finance their expansion, and investors are taken along for the ride.

Acquisitions and partnerships are what individual investors who invest in early stage companies dream of. They get the chance to sell their shares to the acquirer at a premium, or have an inexpensive way into a blue-chip company like Microsoft or Cisco. Most large companies include their new acquisitions directly into existing business divisions. If they don't fit, the parent company might spin them off again at a profit, strengthened but independent, offering investors a second opportunity, this time with some of the risk blunted.

The successful companies at the higher end of the scale have been using their stock as currency to buy the competition in the last several years. Their business model has become what the Japanese call *kiratsu*, lots of joint ventures and establishing relationships.

Paul Cox, manager, St. Louis,
Missouri-based Commerce Bank Mid Cap Fund

When to Buy

It's All a Question of Style

Sometimes I have the patience and other times I want to see the action. I want to move it and shake it. I like to score the home run and I am also disciplined. I don't buy low and sell high. I buy high and sell higher. It works for me.

From the Experienced Investor

All investors dream about finding that mystical moment when a stock has struck rock bottom and is headed for that supernatural spiral to the heights. That's when they want to get in, to strike pay dirt in the modern industrial gold rush. Tipsters make millions publishing newsletters that promise to divulge the moment when all the positive forces converge. The real key to success is perseverance, not psychic ability.

Technology stocks are good buys at any time, but especially in a bull market when general market confidence reinforces the customary confidence in technology. If you are a speculator, you are speculating on how other speculators will speculate, not only on the prospective technology. Investor sentiment is an important part of the investing equation. You are not speculating that the stock will go up, but on the fact that others will say the stock will go up. You speculate not only on the company, but on human psychology.

Technology investors aren't market timers following the cycles of the market, because there are no real cycles in the technology market place. Everything is usually cycling upward. But there are patterns everywhere, and if you look closely enough, you can find a rally across most sectors in December and January. This is known as the January Effect. Over the past three years, the stock market has seen a gain of 15 per cent in this period.

Michael Gianturco, technology columnist for *Forbes* magazine and the author of *How to Buy Technology Stocks* (Little, Brown and Company, 1995), has pinned down the exact best time to buy: it's three o'clock on Monday afternoon in the week of the American Thanksgiving. Monday, typically a down day in any market week, would be the last chance to pick up a bargain before this winter rally begins. He can't pinpoint the reason this happens any more than other pundits can explain the January Effect. But it does happen, and Mr. Gianturco believes it will continue. The year-end rally affects small-cap stocks generally, but it is even more pronounced in the technology sector.

For the brokerage houses, January is like the Christmas season for the retail trade. Much of the activity is concentrated in this one month. There seems to be a mental summing up at the end of the year and a resolve to do better, like an unspoken New Years' resolution. Shortly afterwards with short selling, deferred tax selling, and a cooling-off period, there is a price drop-off. So January in effect gives you the chance to buy and then a chance to sell.

If there is a technology industry slump, and so far there has never really been a major one, the first segment to come back to life is semiconductors, the backbone of the computer. The next to strengthen are the hardware companies, and following along are the software companies. However, the whole sector moves so quickly that you can't wait around for one wave to catch the next.

Short-term investors — day traders — are also looking for cycles that can signal a buy opportunity, and they want to be able to anticipate the upticks and the downturns on a day-to-day basis. Technology stocks usually have good runs for two to three days, then they have to pause and breathe. If a stock is having a good run, you can usually wait for it to fall back a little bit when it starts breathing and maybe buy in at a slightly lower cost.

The Step-Buy Strategy

If I find a stock I like, I would not buy all of it at once. I buy some as it is going up, some a little bit later, some more on a downtick, so you have a relatively decent average price. Then if the stock runs up fast and I've made, say, a 30 per cent return, I'll sell some of the stock off. When I've made 50 per cent, I'll sell another percentage. Fifty per cent in your pocket is better than 75 per cent sitting in the market waiting for a bad news announcement on a Monday morning.

Robert MacLellan, high-tech analyst, Warburg Dillon Read

Being the First to Know:
IPOs and Early-Stage Investing

An Initial Public Offering of a technology company is the most volatile deal in the stock market. As the name implies, an IPO is the first time a company issues its stock to the public. The issue price is set by the underwriter, who considers the amount of capital the company needs to raise, the number of shares being offered to the public, the company's earnings record, as well as the price and earnings of similar companies.

Selling stock to the public gives young companies the money to finance expansion and build brand recognition. Typically an investor can buy a new issue only from the underwriting broker-age firm. If you do not have an account with an underwriting firm, it is hard to buy even a few shares of a new issue, especially if the stock is hot.

If the underwriters think the company will be a huge success, they earmark a lot of the stock for themselves and their firm's best customers in anticipation of a big price increase. If they aren't so sure about the prospects, they won't hold the stock any longer than they have to.

For the individual investor, this is the first chance to hop on the bandwagon. A recent study found that buyers who purchase an IPO at the closing price of its first day, when it first becomes available to most people, earned only about 2 per cent annually, less than if they had left the money in a bank account. Typically an IPO gains about 11 per cent on its day of issue and then after a week it starts to find its level. You have to have the reflexes of a cat and the constitution of a goat to follow the fluctuations up and down, but the risk takers investing in the technology sector always think they do.

An IPO generally underperforms other stocks after going public. If you look just at the Internet-related IPOs, the hottest stocks in the hottest frontier, the investor had the chance of getting in later at less than the offering price on all except Yahoo,

Netscape, and @Home Network. In 1996, high-tech IPOs lost 8.4 per cent of their value compared to the S&P 500, which returned 22.9 per cent over the same period.

Buying an IPO does not even mean getting in on the ground floor of an opportunity. That is where the venture capitalist gets on. At the venture capital stage in Canada, the deals tend to be limited partnerships backed by $150,000 minimum. Just by the nature of the public offering, the venture capitalist has garnered a healthy return for a relatively small investment. Some of the proceeds of the offering go to these original backers. If the deal never goes to public offering, the venture capitalist could lose the whole investment. By the time the individual investor gets to it, the IPO has already been picked over by the venture capitalists and the brokerages' best customers — the institutional investors like pension funds and mutual funds.

Buying an IPO is like buying a new model car in its first year. It still has the kinks and bugs with no history of satisfied drivers behind it. IPOs are rich with promise and cutting-edge technology but short on profits and sales. So who would want them? The same people who would buy the new car. Scoring big with an IPO is the ultimate high for investors who love risk. Because the supply is limited, the hype surrounding a new issue fosters an overwhelming urge to get in early, which often sends the stock price zooming. From Netcom in 1994 to Netscape more recently, the clamour when they entered the market was resounding. Never mind the numbers. If you can score big once, it's worth a whole basket of near misses.

Derivatives, Options, and Other Scary Concepts

As if investing in technology stocks wasn't risky enough, you can make it even riskier. Futures, options, derivatives, shorts, puts, and calls are all risky vehicles, but that may be exactly why investors in the technology sector like them so much. Following the principle of more risk, more reward, you can get very rich very quickly trading options and futures, maybe doubling or tripling your money in a matter of days. Or you can turn a lot of money into very little in a matter of minutes.

You really have to know what you are doing if you are going to trade in options. There are massive volumes analysing and explaining the ins and outs of options, which is somewhat surprising considering that commodity players are not the type to take advice easily. Not wanting to discourage anybody who feels they can handle the risk, here's an introduction to how options work in the technology sector.

An option is a contract giving an investor a right to buy or sell shares of a stock at a specified price, usually today's price, at a later date, usually three, six, or nine months away. An option to buy is known as a call, and the investor is hoping the stock's price will go up. An option to sell is a put and that investor is counting on the price going down by an amount sufficient to provide a profit when he or she sells the option. If the stock price holds steady or moves in the opposite direction, the price paid for the option is lost entirely. A buyer of a call option pays the option writer a fee called a premium. If the option is not exercised before it expires, the premium paid is lost. A buyer of a call option is generally bullish about the underlying security known as the derivative. A writer of a call option usually believes the security or the market will not move up substantially, not making it worthwhile for the buyer to exercise. An option is like a side bet where you win a lot or lose everything.

A future is a contract to buy or sell a prespecified amount of stock at a particular price on an agreed-upon date in the future. Futures differ from options in that the holder of an option has a choice whether or not to exercise the option, but the parties involved in a futures contract are obligated to complete the transaction. You can also buy options on an index of stocks if you believe the sector as a whole is going to go up or down. US technology stock index options trade on the Chicago Board of Options and on the American, Philadelphia, and Pacific stock exchanges.

If you exercise your option and it is called, or put back to you, you have to cover it. The US financial regulator, the Securities and Exchange Commission, is skittish enough about options that it will ask your broker to have you sign documents that certify you know all about option trading, that you like to take risks, and that it's nobody's fault but your own if you lose your shirt.

The other scary type of trade is short selling, which relies on your ability to spot what you consider to be an overvalued stock. It works this way. You borrow the shares from the broker and sell them right away, hoping that others will soon notice what you noticed. When the price comes down, you buy enough shares to pay back your broker and pocket the difference in price. However, if the price goes up, you have to find the money to cover the short position to give the broker back the borrowed stock. When you buy a stock outright, you know that the maximum possible loss is the stock price. If you are selling short and you guessed wrong, you can never tell how much you can lose.

These techniques exaggerate the possible rewards but they also magnify the potential losses. So, if you are considering getting into options and shorting, it is even more important that you know what you are doing.

Triple Witching

Even if you don't play the derivatives, or option markets, they will affect your portfolio. The last hours of the third Friday of March, June, September, and December is the eerie Triple Witching Day. That is the time when futures and options on stock indexes, as well as options on individual stocks, expire simultaneously. Triple Witching is the market's equivalent of a traffic jam with very heavy volume that amplifies any kind of trend already in place. Beginning three or four days before Triple Witching, the market volatility is intense. Although the market is apt to correct itself within the next few days, you may find it sometimes profitable to trade on the volatility before the correction. It is also a signal to the investor about which way and how fast the market is moving.

From the General to the Specific

These are some broad approaches to get a perspective on how to be comfortable analysing the sector as a whole. Now that you have an understanding of the big picture, in the next chapter we are going to zero in on how to find the specific companies that will outperform the sector.

MAKING THE BEST
OF A GOOD THING

The Technology Stock Dating Bar

There are a lot of very romantic people in the market place and there are a great deal of attractive, well-dressed companies coming to market competing for investment dollars.

Loudon Owen, venture capitalist, McLean Watson Capital Inc.

Concept, management, and marketing — those are the three essential ingredients every technology company needs if it is going to succeed. Without a good idea, quality management, and an opportunity for a market, a company is not going to make it, plain and simple. While these factors should be reasonably and clearly explained in prospectuses and brokerage reports, the challenge for the successful investor is the qualitative and creative appraisal of the balance of these essentials. The right stuff that makes up a successful technology company can't be counted. It has to be felt.

Concept

We've all heard the story about the engineers puttering around in the garage or scribbling a diagram on a napkin in a coffee shop and coming up with a concept or product that will revolutionize the world and the way we live. More likely, these guys just happened to be computer science graduates of MIT, Stanford, or the University of Waterloo, used to work for one of the large technology outfits, and snuck an idea that wasn't getting attention out the door. There, they are met by a venture capitalist only too happy to add to his personal fortune by staking these entrepreneurs for, typically, a 40 per cent compounded annual return. Once the product is developed, there is a degree of uncertainty as the market is tested. Now it's time for you, the investor, to step right up and take a chance.

As marketing progresses and shipment begins, the value of the company can be gauged with more certainty at this point. If it's successful, competitors will notice the new product and start working on something similar. A competitor can either ignore the new product, if they don't believe there will be any consequence, go to the trouble and expense of creating a knock-off, or simply buy the technology through acquisition. It is easy enough to reverse-engineer most technologies. Patents and copyright laws are vague enough that most things can be copied at far less cost than inventing them from scratch. Once the same technology is offered by more than one source, since mark-ups are so high, competition brings the price down astronomically and affects the profitability of the company and its stock price. Before a product is actually ready to go to market, the stock price can soar. But many times the ideas just look good on paper, and when the commercial product is finally ready, nobody wants it and it turns out to be a bust. "You have to remember the type of people that are in that technology business tend to be blue-sky-type geniuses and do not give a lot of thought sometimes to 'Does the market want or need this,'" says speculator Ted Carter.

Management

The investor should be able to sense if management has that intangible excitement, that grasp of what's necessary, and that single-mindedness that will distinguish it from the ordinary. One could argue, as some technology purists do, that Microsoft Word wasn't as good a product as WordPerfect, or that IBM never did make a decent PC, but the management of these companies took action and devoted resources to their success. If management has an attitude about their business, a dedication to the details, and an obsession with overcoming their weaknesses, the odds of their success are good.

"We have never lost money investing in smart and honest management," says Neil Nisker of Nisker & Associates Strategic Growth Management. "They are the driving force of the company. They own the source code, they invented the product, and it is their vision you are buying into."

As a comparison to technology, the banks are very process-oriented institutions. Everything proceeds through a well-established procedure. In technology, there's a mixture of process and intuition. Management needs a sense of the market, a sense of the advertising message, and a sense of finding the right feelings to transmit about the company to command loyalty from their customers and employees. It is much more personal. It's much less institutionalized and much less processed. It's much more intuitive.

Good management is leadership with vision and strategic thinking, and the ability to inspire others to fulfil that vision. "One of the questions I ask myself when I meet a CEO," Trimark manager Rick Serafini says, "is would I want to work for this person? Do the people who work there believe in the vision? Would he or she allow the people below them the freedom and independence to execute the vision. What's the culture in the company?"

Examining the company's management is a way to determine, guess really, what its potential is in the market place. And if it's a one-man show and that person drops dead, could it mean trouble?

And When I Die...

The question I posed to Terry Matthews, the CEO of Newbridge Network Corp., was what happens if you're hit by a bus and are no longer able to operate as the supersalesman. He said, 'We have very strong department heads who could carry on directing the company, as well as filling the sales shoes.' There would be a different make-up to the company, but the company would certainly be able to continue without Terry Matthews.

Robert McWhirter, vice president and technology portfolio manager, Royal Bank Investment Management

In many cases, the first heads of technology start-ups are the inventors. While they bring a lot of early enthusiasm to the company, inventors generally do not make good managers over the long run. "Technical people enamoured with the bits and the bytes, tend to jump on every new technology bandwagon and hype it as nirvana," Warburg Dillon Read technology analyst Robert MacLellan says. "And that is never, ever, ever the case. It's so easy to get overwhelmed by tech think and lose focus of other issues you're supposed to look at as part of doing research, like management attitude and capabilities, strategic positions, and financial health."

It's a long jump from engineer to entrepreneur, and when you reach a certain critical mass, business acumen is much more vital than technical know-how. As a rule, investors in early-stage companies should look for professional managers with prior experience in running technology companies. Technology companies have their own peculiar needs.

"It's very difficult for inventors, or one-man shops, to take the company to the next stage," says Edward Jamieson, research and portfolio manager for Franklin Resources Inc. of San Mateo, California. "A good venture investor will usually make sure to install a management team to go with the product. I don't know what the empirical or academic research would say about this, but when a company gets to about $100 million in sales, it's a very critical juncture in its development. A lot of companies get to $100 million and that's it. They just seem to hit a wall. They just don't seem to be able to go beyond it. It's a time to be very careful."

A professional manager, especially one who has been there before with a technology company, has a bigger vision than the inventor. While the inventor is proud to hold his dream in his hands, the professional manager can fit the invention into the bigger scheme of things and spin it out into a family of products. In the chapter on networking, I will tell you the story of Cisco and how it grew.

"If it ends up being twice as big as they thought, they are just rolling in clover," Hambrecht &Quist's senior technology analyst, Doug van Dorsten, says. "They decide we are doing great and let's keep doing this. The professional manager would say, 'You are addressing a market that is 15 or 20 times as big, and if you do the following this company will be not twice as big next year, but 10 times, and in two or three years, it could be huge.'"

Who is in charge of the company can tell a potential investor about the direction in which it is headed. If the inventor can recognize the benefits of sacrificing control so that an experienced manager can ensure that the company can continue to rise in revenues, an important juncture has been crossed.

Likely winners in the technology market should be able to give convincing answers to two key questions:

1. **Can the company capitalize on burgeoning global demand?** According to management consultants McKinsey and Company, the United States in 1984 accounted for 57 per cent of the world market for computer hardware, but by 1994, that was down to 40 per cent and dropping. The companies with a future are the ones that know how to sell globally.

2. **Does the company partner well?** According to partnering master John Chambers, CEO of Cisco Systems, "Companies that don't do joint ventures, and learn how to acquire, get left behind."

This is an industry where the difference between good and bad management is the difference between making a lot of money and losing all your money. You're playing in a fluid, dynamic industry where things are happening rapidly and management has to keep a grip on the business.

Brian Ashford-Russell, co-manger,
Mackenzie World Science and Technology Fund

Questions to Ask

John Drolet, Yorkton Securities senior analyst, asks these questions about management when he is evaluating a company's chances of success:

1. Is management credible?

2. What is management's background and expertise?

3. Do the managers know what they are talking about?

4. Have the managers formulated a good business plan?

5. Have the managers assessed how much competition there is?

6. What is management's strategy to deal with companies that can crush them?

7. Has management assessed the company's niche?

8. How will management keep the company big enough to grow, but small enough to keep the big guys uninterested?

Why Management Counts

What do you look at when you are investing in a bank? Do you look at the CEO? You don't care about him because the value of the company is in its assets. In a technology company, the assets are brains. It's a completely different way of valuing a company.

Gaylen Duncan, president and CEO,
Information Technology Association of Canada (ITAC)

Also not to be overlooked is the composition of the board of directors. Rick Serafini likes an independent board with the majority of the members coming from outside the company, but he wants at least some of the board members to have gone through the pain of a high-growth company experience. Most technology company boards, he grumbles, are comprised of a lawyer, a broker, a couple of people from the inside, and some politicians. "That is a huge warning sign. I personally would not invest in a company with that sort of board make-up."

Marketing

Marketing, marketing, marketing is the mantra you hear in the technology industry. It's similar to the location, location, location chant of the retail and real estate industries. No matter how good the technology is, to most investors, the ability to get the product to market has to be even better. It is not enough for the research and development to be good; the distribution channels have to be outstanding.

Apple Computer, for instance, has a tough time getting its products accepted in the corporate environment, except for the graphics and engineering departments. Corel's PerfectOffice has found acceptance in the retail channels but can't crack Microsoft Office's corporate stranglehold. In fact, Microsoft has captured the word-processing market from Corel, the spreadsheet market from Lotus, and the database market from Borland through its distribution domination. Now Microsoft is challenging Netscape in the browser market. Netscape is using a form of shareware to get its product to market, while Microsoft is bundling its browser with its other market-leading products.

With today's bright idea quickly becoming yesterday's anachronism, being first to market is an important part of the ability to dominate it. The market changes so rapidly that the life cycle of a technology product could be as short as six months. With the opportunity to dominate so time sensitive, the investor is always looking for companies that not only are first to market, but have the ability to come up with follow-up products.

Good technology is not even 50 per cent of the equation. Some technology areas move so quickly that even if you are first out of the door with the best technology, if you can't keep pace with the industry, you quickly find your new technology is old technology.

Robert Millham, analyst, C. M. Oliver & Company

Dell Computers, and later Gateway 2000, both superb stock performers, perfected the direct order method of marketing their products through mail order or phone order. It allows them to take the order, customize the system for the customer's needs, and ship it quickly via UPS or Federal Express. By cutting down on inventory and overhead costs, these companies are able to offer competitive prices and still maintain their margins.

Compaq Computer Corp., the world's largest personal computer manufacturer, sells its computers through its corporate sales force and an extensive dealer and distributor network. Taking aim at the lean operations and low prices of its fast-growing competitors, it is adding a direct sale stream to its distribution strategy.

Regis McKenna, Technology's Marketing Guru

If investors who feel that marketing is key to the success of technology products had followed Regis McKenna into new ventures, they would be moving from triumph to triumph. The Silicon Valley consultant has basically redefined high-technology marketing. He helped launch innovations for the most important technology companies, including the first microprocessor for Intel, the first personal computer for Apple, the first recombinant DNA genetically engineered product for Genentech Inc., and the first retail computer store. The technology venture capital firm Kleiner Perkins Caufield & Byers (KPCB) has invested $961 million in 240 privately held companies and taken 76 of them public, including Compaq, Sun Microsystems, Symantec, Lotus, Intuit, and Netscape, and they continue to hit the jackpot. The partners at KPCB call on McKenna's services every time they fund a new venture.

Regis McKenna turned the business-school marketing model on its ear. Traditionally, companies would develop a product in secret, make it, announce it, and ship it. Regis McKenna influenced Microsoft to follow a different marketing timetable: first announce the product, then design it, then make it, and finally sell it. With one announcement, Microsoft alters the pricing structure and marketing strategy for an entire sector. Its competitors are thrown into a frenzy just by the threat that Microsoft might invade their territory. The consumer appetite is whetted by what is known in the industry as "vaporware," a product that is still the figment of someone's imagination. The vaporware strategy generates a double whammy. Investors are attracted when the announcement is made, and the investment excitement builds again when the product is shipped.

So the well-connected investor can choose to cash in on the concept-hot engineers, like Gordon Moore and Robert Noyce, who left Shockley Labs for Fairchild Semiconductor, and then went on to found Intel. Or he can follow a hot manager, like Tom Mitchell, who founded Seagate Technology Inc. in 1979, Conner Peripherals Inc. in 1986, and JTS Corp. in 1994. Or he can peg his investment selection to the hottest marketer, like Regis McKenna. The best bet might be to go with the package of concept, management, and marketing put together by astute venture capitalists like Kleiner Perkins Caufield and Byers.

Keeping Good People

One of the things I look for in a technology company is do they have Golden Handcuffs. The guys who are the key assets of the company I want to load with options and warrants exercisable two or three years from now so they are tied there. In a bank, I want management to all to have Golden Parachutes. I want to them to be phasing out the older guys.

Gaylen Duncan, president and CEO, ITAC

An automobile company has to have a plant and facilities in place before it can grow, even if the demand for the product is there. Since most technology companies are limited only by how fast they can recruit good people; there is no lag time in their growth potential. A company like Netscape can sustain immediate rapid growth simply by adding people and installing them into leased space. There is no need to wait to build a factory. Most competitive technology companies use a similar efficient flat business model. They lease facilities and hire people as they need them.

Technology is a business of intellectual property and, it is said, the assets walk out the door every night. You can't force people to stay as a company grows but investors want the key individuals in the company to have a real personal commitment and an enormous incentive not to leave. Silicon Valley has embraced stock options to attract, retain, and reward talented employees. New technology companies promise stock to their key employees at low prices as compensation enticement. For example, more than 20 per cent of the Microsoft shares are set aside as stock-related incentives.

Options and ownership incentives may be good for the employees but they are a mixed blessing for investors. Stock options began as a way to lower the initial costs for a start-up company, and shareholders liked them because they aligned the interest of employees with that of the shareholders. By rewarding them for their achievements options gave them an incentive to work hard and commit to the economic success of the enterprise. Now that these companies are maturing, some stockholders are debating whether stock options are a good investment or a waste of company assets. These dissenters feel that stock option programs are transferring large sums of wealth from the shareholders to insiders, and shifting the voting power that goes along with these shares. They also feel that employees given stock options pay so little for the shares they are risking less than outside investors who pay full price. While stock options lower compensation costs early on, critics think technology companies are too generous in this regard.

"There is nothing like a culture where people are sharing in the success of the company, working 18 hours a day. and loving it because they are getting rich," says Trimark money manager Rick Serafini. "But it's a bad thing, diluting the other shareholders."

"Three per cent of the equity in options is probably OK for a fast-growing, well-managed company that needs a lot of really smart engineers and sales people," says Paul Wick, manager of the Seligman Communications and Information Fund. "More than 3 per cent gets excessive and the company is diluting its public shareholders."

Employee stock options have become the *modus operandi* in Silicon Valley. When times are good, stock options are a real incentive and the entrepreneurial spirit is strong. But when times are tougher and the stock price is sinking (and all companies go through up and down cycles, especially growth companies), the company is vulnerable. Employees know that their friends, the engineers down the valley, are doing well and their companies are offering a thousand more options to talented people. Meanwhile, they also know that their own products are late, their stock is going down, and their stock options are under water. They begin to jump ship.

Hambrecht & Quist's Checklist

Hambrecht & Quist (H&Q), founded in 1968, is considered by many to be the number one investment bank specializing in the technology sector. By limiting its focus, H&Q has developed an understanding of the dynamics of investing in these growth companies and identifying emerging-growth opportunities. Here's how Hambrecht & Quist senior technology analyst Doug van Dorsten assesses a technology company's potential:

"We look for companies that:

- have good products;

- have a good management;

- have a good performance record;

- have fairly consistent operating models;

- have stable growth from quarter to quarter;

- are pretty predictable, without a great deal of fluctuation in gross profit margin;

- demonstrate good fiscal discipline;

- don't have excess inventory;

- don't spend a lot of money on plant and equipment;

- don't owe too much or have too much owed to them."

Building an Empire

A software company has to be perverse to spend money on things. Software companies don't have inventory and they don't need a lot in the way of hard assets. It would take the CEO building a monument to himself to erect a plant that wasn't efficient. If you have a software code that doesn't work very well, you update it and you're only out the cost of diskettes or the CD-ROM. Big deal, it doesn't matter.

Douglas van Dorsten,
senior technology analyst, Hambrecht & Quist

Bram Kirshner's Buying Opportunities

The technology stock market has been very good to individual investor Bram Kirshner. He follows the market every day, usually making at least a couple of trades. Even focusing his atention on the market, he is dazzled at how fast things can move. Although he is still amazed at how quickly value can slip away in a technology stock, he doesn't let that faze him. He sees it as a buying opportunity. "I make most of my money when I buy a stock and it goes down," he says. "I reassess it and often what I like is still there, only it's cheaper." This is what Bram Kirshner sees as a buying opportunity:

1. **A company with an excellent track record over a three- to five-year period experiencing short-term operational problems.** In Wall Street terms, that means missing quarterly earning projections, which for some companies can mean a price dip of up to 50 per cent, depending on the market environment. If he is comfortable with management's long-term goals, and if the forward opportunity is big enough, he'll step up and buy.

2. **A company going through a management change or a change in strategy.** He has to feel comfortable with the new management team and its vision. Companies going through changes are unlikely to be profitable or they wouldn't be doing it. Kirshner wants to see a plan in place to get back to profitability over the next four or five quarters, which is how long he thinks a turnaround should take.

3. **A company with the same management team going through a transition period.** He is prepared for two or three quarters of losses while they solve their problems. After two or three good quarters, he expects momentum investors to move in and push the price back up.

Consulting Companies

One of the dangers of investing in technology stocks is the risk of obsolescence. Despite the fact that existing companies are churning out new innovative products, somebody in a garage or attic somewhere might be making one that's better, stronger, and faster. One thing that never changes style and benefits from anybody's technology growth is the technology consulting services. As one of its larger holdings, the Mackenzie Universal World Science and Technology Fund has favoured Gartner Group Inc. with headquarters in Stamford, Connecticut, one of the leading advisory services or consultants on information technology. Companies around the world are spending $600 billion a year on information technology and estimates are that this will grow to $1.3 trillion by 2000. As a percent of revenue, spending on information technology is expected to increase from 5.8 percent in 1995 to 9.2 percent in the year 2000.

Gartner Group first went public in 1986 until it was acquired 1988 by Saatchi & Saatchi. In 1990, there was a management takeover that involved a partnership with Dun & Bradstreet. Gartner Group went public again in October 1993, and issued 21.6 million shares at $2.75 per share (split adjusted), for total gross proceeds of $53.9 million. Its revenues have increased by four times in five years.

Like its competitors, the Meta Group, Forrester Research, Intelliquest Information Group, and the Yankee Group, Gartner helps businesses make technology decisions, such as which accounting software system they should use and what database vendor has the best product for their needs. Five or 10 years ago, the technology decisions were simple enough to be left to an internal MIS director. Now, with an ever-increasing portion of the capital spent by corporations going into technology, the choice of technology is a critical strategic decision, and the decisions are being outsourced to consultants such as Gartner. "I like the company for a couple of reasons," says Jim Broadfoot, co-manager of the Mackenzie Science and Technology Fund. "As the strategic importance evolves, the value added by a consultant increases."

As its business model, Gartner Group uses a subscription model with high renewal rates. Clients pay 12 months in advance, cash up front and revenue flows through on a monthly basis, so the company is always sure what its projected revenues will be. It can set its costs accordingly and hedge against any anticipated risk. Information about technology is in constant flux. As a result, a customer who signs a contract with Gartner Group will renew year after year in order to stay abreast of what is going on in the industry. More than 90 per cent of Gartner's client base renew, giving them a nice stream of predictable income. As with the other consulting companies, Gartner's main overhead expense is its staff of researchers, giving the company operating margins over 20 per cent and revenue growth over 35 per cent. The company trades at more than 11 times sales and 63 times forward earnings.

In contrast, semiconductor manufacturers, as an example, are constantly buffeted by changes of inventory in the channel and the risk that a competitor could leapfrog and have a new product to market sooner. "As a fund manager with a lot of exposure to risk, I need a stable kind of business like the Gartner Group for balance, and if I was an individual investor, I would look for that stabilization as well," says Jim Broadfoot.

Finding Companies Being Revitalized by Technology

Some astute investors are cashing in on the technology boom by looking for opportunities where technology is revitalizing moribund industries or companies. Some companies — like Dupont, General Electric, and Monsanto — have shifted their corporate direction directly into new technologies. Monsanto has completely changed its business focus from chemicals to biotechnology with very positive repercussions on its stock price. Monsanto's price strength is attributed to the spin-off of its long-established chemical business, which was affected by economic cycles and driven by the price of its supplies. The biotech business, on the other hand, is perceived to have growth potential. If biotechnology was spun off, analysts say, the new company would have a higher valuation than Monsanto as a whole.

Look at some other industries and see how technology has made them attractive again:

Airlines

In the airline industry, the challenge is to fill the seats as efficiently as possible and maximize the capacity of the airline fleet. The better market performers have sophisticated software programs to track ticket sales. American Airlines, for example, makes more money from incorporating other airlines on its SABRE computerized reservations system than it does from frequent flyers. Using technology to calculate the logarithms to adequately, but not too generously, schedule the crews and aircraft for a sunny Monday before a long weekend can dramatically influence a company's bottom line. With the right technology, an airline can project, and not guess, how many people will fly, where they will fly, and the ratio of overbooking to actual use.

Banking

Increasingly banking is no longer physically taking place in a traditional bank branch. With the increased functionality of ATM machines and the latest twists in telecommunications and the Internet, banking technology has become a competitive weapon for the banks. Trimark Trust in Toronto allows the consumer to acquire a mortgage using technology without having to physically sit in a chair and talk to someone. By not having to pay someone to review the loan in person, Trimark can offer a mortgage at a rate one-eighth to one-quarter of a per cent better than the competition. Even at a lower rate, its profit margin outperforms its competitors.

Couriers

Purolator Courier Ltd. has a number of convenient drop boxes in large cities for customers to deposit their packages. Drivers cruise the city by night, stopping and opening every box to check for parcels. However, a wireless transmitter is being developed that will allow the driver to detect if there is actually anything in the drop box. If the transmitter doesn't detect anything, the driver can drive to the next box on the route without ever having to stop.

Vending Machines

A similar wireless transmitter is in the works to make the servicing of vending machines more efficient by detecting if a particular product is running low. The machine can be restocked before it actually runs out thereby increasing customer satisfaction, revenue and profitability for the operator. "Literally every day there is a new method of installing technology to make something faster, better, cheaper," says Robert McWhirter of Royal Bank Investment Management.

The most important point of any investment is the entry point, and the next most important point is the exit point. As Cameron Groome, First Marathon Securities Limited's biotechnology analyst, says, "it's fun when you are in early and out early," The next chapter will reveal the selling secret.

WHEN TO SELL:
BREAKING UP
IS HARD TO DO

Don't Get Greedy

If a stock's going through the roof, there will always be people who want to buy it. They may make more money than you, but you have to bear in mind that they can lose it as easily. If you're basically an individual investor, investing your college fund or your retirement fund or your mad money, you set percentage return rates and don't get greedy.

Robert MacLellan, high-tech analyst, Warburg Dillon Read

As hard as it is to figure out when to buy a stock, it's even harder to know when to sell. Psychologically, they say, selling is the hardest thing in the world. It's much more difficult for investors to force themselves to sell a losing stock than to sell a winner. Egos are on the line. Nobody likes to admit they have made a mistake, and when you sell a losing stock, you are telling the world.

A professional money manager has an additional incentive when it comes to selling. Sure his ego is at stake when he sells, but if he holds on, his clients will get a statement at the end of the quarter showing all the dogs he picked for the portfolio. Since he doesn't want anyone to know he was dumb enough to buy the dog, he'll sell it, even if he still believes in it, so it doesn't besmirch his record.

There is no absolute correct moment to sell. But it is better to sell too soon than too late. The technology sector is a hard market for market timers since it follows its own rhythms. So selling at the top and buying at the bottom is an extraordinary feat. "You want to get your initial investment back and move on to other things with the money you've made," Yorkton Securities analyst John Drolet says. "If you overstay your welcome, you could be in trouble."

The Stop Loss

On the downside, investors can put in stop losses. As we have seen in Chapter 2, a stop loss is an order to the broker to sell when the stock falls by a certain percentage, or to a certain point. If you put in a stop loss of 15 per cent, and the stock trades badly, the stock will be sold, and you'll only lose 15 per cent. A stop loss is a discipline. It reminds you about your first expectation, and if you change your mind, it forces you to actually do something actively to rescind the stop-loss order instead of just letting it ride.

But in the technology sector, a stock can fall a significant amount within one day and then correct again. You have to force yourself to revisit and rethink your objectives every so often so you don't get taken out too easily. A stop-loss order can kick in just when the investor wants to stay the course and ride the volatility.

One trick is to set your stop-loss order at odd numbers — like $16 or $21 rather than $15 or $20 — because most investors have stop loss orders that kick in at round numbers. But when the computers start the automatic sell-off and volumes soar, the stock can rebound dramatically.

Hitting the Road

When does one think about taking profits and moving on? What do you do if you have invested in a company in an undeveloped market sector where there's been rapid growth and no direct competition, and suddenly you start seeing more direct competition? You have to make a clear-headed assessment about where the market is headed. You could decide the period of explosive growth is at an end and it's time to move on to another sector, especially if a company like Microsoft is the competitor. Or you could decide that competition heralds the maturing of that market and offers a level of legitimacy it did not have before. Exclusive markets in which there is suddenly competition can continue to grow at a very rapid pace, and investors should move on only if there's another opportunity that looks better elsewhere.

Networking is a good example of that. Five years ago, there was very little direct competition to Cisco in the business of selling switches, hubs, and routers. Today, there is a lot of direct competition in this sector, and a lot of consolidation, yet Cisco continues to grow at a rapid pace. Had an investor in Cisco taken the view that competition signalled the time to move on, she would have missed an opportunity to substantially increase her net worth.

People who have thought about the market say that there is only one reason to sell, and that is if you can find better value. Neil Nisker of Nisker & Associates Strategic Growth Management sells his losers before he will sell his winners. But, he warns, you have to compare apples and apples. The investor with money in technology has to ask if there is better value within the sector. "A lot of people believe that once you have doubled or tripled your money you should sell. We ask, does the company continue to have the potential to grow? As long as the answer is positive, we will continue to hold."

Behave Yourself

A stock has a personality. You begin to sense when the stock is being moody. It's kind of like when a mother knows the difference between the cry of her child when the child is hungry or wet. As an investor, you acquire this sense and you can tell when a stock's run is over.

From the Experienced Investor

Technology is a market which is full of surprises. It's difficult to calculate when growth stocks will reach full value. It's a moving target. When you think a stock couldn't possibly go any higher, it does. When five or 10 times appreciation is a realistic possibility, it is not easy to set a goal. "Most small investors will hold on to their losers because they have no idea how to value whether it's going to come back or not. So they just keep praying it's going to come back. I'll sell a loser in a minute," investor Bram Kirshner says. "In technology, it's amazing how quickly value can slip away. I owned Gandalf Technologies Inc. just when ISDN [the Integrated Services Digital Network standard for providing both voice and data services over a regular phone line] was catching on. Gandalf was a player in ISDN for a brief moment. I was lucky enough to catch the trend and the stock shot off like a rocket. And I was lucky I got out."

The Shareholder's Lament

In 1995, I went in for 100 shares of a company that intrigued me. Then it began a process of self-destruction right before my eyes. It was one of those classic situations where I couldn't believe that it would not bounce back at some point. I wasn't as disciplined as I am now, so I wasn't prepared to take a little bit of pain. So I took a whole lot of pain and I just sold it for $9.50. And I had paid $44. It hurt, and that taught me a lesson.

From the Experienced Investor

The flip side is that technology investors often find themselves getting out of a stock when they feel the time is right, but then it does bounce back and they find themselves getting back in many points higher. There's nothing wrong with that. Circumstances change and the prospects for a stock might become clearer as it goes up. Investors want to get the maximum reward, but they also want to mitigate the risk.

Sell Signals

It would be great if we could come up with a formula for successfully divesting. In any publicly traded company, you can watch the volume matched with the price. But the fundamentals of the company are the most important thing. Somewhat secondary are whether or not the company's sector, whether it is mining or technology, is in favour, because that will ebb and flow.

Loudon Owen, venture capitalist, McLean Watson Capital Inc.

Five Good Reasons to Sell

1. **An adverse management change**. New management is not necessarily good management.

2. **Declining profit margins**. One bad quarter doesn't mean trouble, but it is a reason to have a good look at what caused the problem.

3. **A deteriorating financial condition**. If a company has suddenly taken on too much debt, it could be a sign of trouble.

4. **Competition**. Nobody has a monopoly on a good idea. When others see the potential and enter the business and start cutting prices and eroding earnings, it may be time to move on.

5. **Dependence on a single product**. In the 1960s, Brunswick Corporation was viewed as a growth stock. Its technology was an automatic bowling-pin machine and every bowling facility in the world made sure to buy it. But once the equipment was installed, growth slowed.

Five Bad Reasons to Sell

1. **The price hasn't moved**. Patience is a virtue. If the fundamentals remain attractive, it's worth the wait.

2. **A paper loss**. A stock might be worth keeping in a declining market.

3. **A paper profit**. Even if you hit a four-bagger, if the fundamentals show that it is still worth having, hold on to it.

4. **Temporary bad news**. A bad quarter doesn't necessarily mean there is anything wrong with the company. Something else might have gone wrong.

5. **You're looking for more action**. Not every day has to be a national holiday. Some days are just good days.

The Trader

There are people who trade once a quarter, people who trade once a month, and people who trade once or twice a day. Whereas one type of trader might want to buy a stock for the next quarter or the next year, another trader would have a number of trades on the block list to do today. What I call a trading account would be a once-a-year trade. My personal opinion is that the most money is made with a minimum holding period of a year.

Cameron Groome,
biotechnology analyst, First Marathon Securities Ltd.

If other investors start bailing out of a stock for no apparent reason, there is a natural tendency to believe they know something that you don't. That's not always the case. Sometimes it's the madness of the crowd. Charles MacKay, in his classic book *Extraordinary Popular Delusions and the Madness of Crowds*, first published in 1841, writes about Tulipomania in Holland in 1624, when tulip bulbs traded at a higher price than gold. Tulips, a new technology introduced into Europe from Turkey in the 16th century, were the objects of wild financial speculation in Holland. After years of speculation, Dutch tulip prices collapsed and hundreds of people were ruined as the bottom fell out of the market. Some people say the Great Crash of 1929, junk bonds of the '80s, and overvalued high-tech stocks of the 1990s are twentieth-century aberrations similar to Tulipomania.

In some cases, a bailout does mean the beginning of the end for a company. However, in the technology sector, a sharp downturn for no reason could just as easily be a short-term retraction. It might, in fact, represent a perfect buying opportunity. As always, the key thing about knowing when to get out involves doing your homework before you get in. That way, if you make the drastic decision to buy again at a lower price, the odds are better that you made the right decision. ""I guess the biggest thing is not to over-react," Warburg Dillon Read analyst Robert MacLellan says. "While that's easy to say, it's hard to do. There is very much a lemming-type mentality in the market, the herd mentality. Sometimes the herd moves for some intelligent reason. Sometimes it doesn't."

Investor, Know Thyself

Whenever I trade, I put myself on the opposite side. When I'm buying, I'm asking myself why is this person selling to me. If I'm selling, I'm asking why do they want to buy from me. Then I ask myself, is this panic? Is there something going on? When you begin to think like that, you get a better sense of your own strength and weaknesses and how you trade.

From the Experienced Investor

There are other triggers to look for in a fundamental analysis of when to sell. If you look at the balance sheet and see account receivables growing faster than the top line, that should be a cause for worry. In the technology sector, companies have a ten-dency to ship product in the current quarter to show positive revenue growth. Then they take back the units shipped as returns in the next quarter.

"One thing professional investors key in on and pay a great deal of attention to is DSOs — day sales outstanding — or, as they are known in other industries, receivables," says Jim Broadfoot, co-manager of the Mackenzie World Science and Technology Fund. "Analysts give DSOs tremendous scrutiny in every quarter-ly report, and if a company's DSOs are up, it often means there has been shelf stuffing. Product gets shipped out at the end of a quarter so the company can achieve its projected quarterly number. But, of course, the more they ship, the more likely they are to miss the next quarter."

Companies making excuses for missing growth projections, slow development, and late release of new products should also be big warning signs. Missing these numbers can mean the company is going through a bad product transition or that its competitors have a better product. However, if growth projections are missed, don't automatically assume the worst. It is best to determine if the problem is specific to the company or industry-wide, especially if the company is making excuses.

One Man's Selling Strategy

• Whether you are talking about technology or any other sector of the market, it's important to let winners ride. I am always reluctant to sell a stock just because it's done well. I will trim back if the stock is going up a lot, but as long as the fundamentals seem to be on track, I want to keep some exposure. It always seems like winners do better than you think they possibly can, and losers slip more than you think they could. So, to make that work in your favour, you try to get as much mileage as you can out of winners.

• On the other hand, when the original investment seems to be turning sour and you no longer have confidence in it, then you want to be quick to sell.

• Turnarounds always take longer than you think, particularly in technology. Often they don't happen, and the risk that you run is that you have a lot of dead wood piling up in your portfolio while you are waiting for them to happen.

Jim Broadfoot, chief investment officer,
Mackenzie Investment Management Inc.

The selling discipline has to match the realities of the market place. The volatility of the sector also warrants more frequent review of the investment, perhaps on a monthly, or at least a quarterly, basis. If you experience substantial gains, it's always prudent to do risk reduction, which means selling off part of your holding as the stock appreciates until you have earned back your original investment and you are now playing with the market's money.

Words to Live By

You have to realize that the odds are stacked against you. The first thing to do after you've bought a stock is to get your original investment out as quickly as possible, no matter how much you believe in the technology. When the stock dangles at a particular price level for any period of time, and it can't seem to break through to the next level, and you start to see more and more selling, sell half of your core holding as well. The odds are that the stock is going into a period of doldrums where it will start to drift down. While the technology might still be good, it's just the boring period. People don't want to hang around for the next eight or 10 months waiting for the next announcement of another breakthrough. They want to go where the action is. If you really believe in the technology, hold that core part, and expand or reduce that as time goes on.

Ted Carter, editor, Carter's Choice newsletter

How Not to Fall in Love

For some investors — men especially — playing the stock market is like a visit to an old-fashioned hardware store. There are so many marvellous gadgets and doodads and you have to try every one of them. When you get them home, some are very useful but others languish in your workshop forever. Technology stocks can have the same effect on you, but unlike the hardware store, where all sales are usually final, the stock market lets you sell them back when they are no longer useful to you. Even if you continue to admire a company and its products, you can still be prepared to sell it. Just because it made substantial gains for you, you don't owe it anything. When the time comes to cut loose, let it go without regret, or you might have something to regret later.

It helps to remind yourself that when you are buying shares in a company you are not buying the great new technology itself. Your money isn't benefiting the plucky and talented inventor. He has gotten his money from the underwriters already. This is a commercial transaction. You are buying from somebody who thinks that you are paying more than the share is worth and you are selling to somebody who thinks they are getting a bargain.

Stocks are made to be bought and sold. If you fall in love and hold on too long, you might find yourself in a trading range that is too tight for comfort. Analysts watch trading ranges — a stock's highest and lowest price over a specified time — because they believe it is significant when a security breaks out of its range at either the high or low end and new targets have been set. When things are going well, you want them to keep going well. When they stop going well, that's when you want to cut the ties.

"Don't fall in hate with a company either. They can come back and they can come back with a vengeance," says Cameron Groome, First Marathon's biotechnology analyst. "Look at Biovail Corporation. That company was going to go bankrupt. They turned it around and they're having a great success. Most people missed it because they had the perception it was at death's door."

How to Know You Have Reached the Top

When your taxi driver and your neighbour start telling you to buy, that's usually a good indicator you are at the top. This sector is very momentum-oriented, and once it gets hot, it just keeps on getting hot, hot, hot. As the momentum runs out, it's like boom! The bottom drops out. If you buy at the top, you are basically finished.

Richard Woo, high-tech analyst,
Thomson Kernaghan & Company Limited

Selling signals aren't always that easy to decipher. The reason for retreating is sometimes the same as the reason for standing your ground and the subtlety in knowing the difference is slim. Even experienced investors season their portfolios with technology mutual funds and let professional money managers solve those double-edged riddles. More and more individuals without the time or inclination to follow their investments through the ups and downs are counting on professionals in whom they have confidence. In the next chapter, we see how they think.

MUTUAL FUNDS:
SAFETY IN NUMBERS

A mutual fund is an institutionalized way of putting many stocks into a basket or bundle. It is worth paying attention to what the professional managers are doing, even for investors who prefer to invest on their own. A professional fund manager with expertise and resources is watching those stocks every day, while you go to work to earn more money to invest in the stock market. The manger is constantly being informed of opportunities and information that an individual investor couldn't possibly have access to. By bundling, you eliminate some of the risk associated with this sector although it is never entirely without risk.

According to BellCharts Inc, a mutual fund tracking service, at the end of 1997 there were 15 mutual funds specializing in the technology sector available in Canada. The only one with a record longer than 10 years is the Hyperion Science and Technology Fund, now the Talvest/Hyperion Global Science and Technology Fund, with assets of $10 million. The next oldest, Green Line's Science and Technology Fund, shows returns of over 30 per cent over three years. And just as an indication of how quickly interest in this sector has grown, Altamira Service and Technology Fund is the only other one that has been around longer than one year.

In the United States, with its bigger market, there are 55 science and technology funds: 15 have five-year records, 12 have 10-year records. They range from small to large, with the best performers being Fidelity Select Computer and Select Electronics Funds, Seligman Communications and Information Fund, and the grandaddy of technology funds, the 10-year-old T. Rowe Price Science and Technology Fund.

Who Are the Fund Managers?

Most people shopping for a mutual fund check out how it has done in the past, looking back at performances over one year, five years, and ten years. But one of the saws of the investment business is that you can't always judge a fund by its history. In this sector, history is definitely no way to differentiate. To get a sense of how a fund will perform in both good and bad markets, you need three years to account for more than one complete economic cycle. With their short time horizon, most technology fund managers probably haven't had that long a track record to trade on, so one has to look at experience that relates to technology.

Jim Broadfoot, for instance, co-manager of the new Mackenzie Universal World Science and Technology Fund, is best known for managing the successful Universal US Emerging Growth Fund. Because technology is decidedly a growth sector, he thinks his handling of the growth fund is a good measure of how he will do with technology. "The Emerging Growth Fund has a significant component in technology," he says. "If I were running a fund that specialized in large-cap value stocks, I don't think there would be much transferability of skills."

It is worthwhile for investors to take into account the investing philosophy of the fund managers. If you want to take a flyer, and the managers want to play it safe, you are obviously in the wrong fund. With the situation in technology changing so quickly, the hands-on approach of the manager means a lot more than it does in any other mutual fund portfolio.

If a fund is performing well, the fund manager is likely to use the new money he or she will naturally attract to the fund to buy more of his or her winners. If the fund becomes big enough, heavy buying by the fund is going to affect the momentum of its stock holdings and the fund will perform even better. However, it then becomes harder to react quickly to changes in the market since selling can radically push down the value of the stocks the fund is trying to unload.

The ideal background for a fund manager is a combination of experience in the technology industry and in finance, either with an MBA, a CFA, or a CA. If the manager has been in the technology business, he or she should have recent enough experience to know the players, yet he or she removed enough to judge the finances without being influenced by the halo of seductive technology.

The psychology is different in the technology sector than any other sector. You have to be aware of the risks in each of the companies you invest in. It is very labour-intensive.

Brian Ashford-Russell, manager, Henderson Investors

Things to Ask About the Technology Fund Managers

1. What were they doing for a living before they did this?

2. What did they cover before they covered technology?

3. Are they so technologically focused that they lose focus of the financial and the management side?

Diversification

Let's face it. It is very hard to identify the next Microsoft, Intel, or Cisco. Everybody wants to hit the big home run, and by diversifying through a mutual fund, you have a better chance of finding one. You reduce the risk and volatility and achieve some stability. But hopefully, with the skill and experience of the mutual fund manager, the portfolio will include The Next Big One.

Odds are that in any particular bundle of technology stocks, two out of five are going nowhere, one is going to go bankrupt, and the other two will perhaps end up giving an above-average return. Historically, the return from the winners has been more than the loss from the losers. With luck, one of the winners your fund manager chooses will be the one that goes over the top.

Other Mutual Fund Strategies

Mutual funds have a natural bias towards larger-cap stocks because of their need for liquidity. To their advantage, the overwhelming returns in the technology sector lately have come from the big players. As a portfolio manager, Ian Ainsworth, manager of the Altamira Science and Technology Fund, says he is monitored, or benchmarked, against the various technology indices which are also weighted towards large-cap high-performance companies like Microsoft, Cisco, and Intel.

"You have to be conscious of the large-cap nature of the benchmark you're trying to compete with," he says. "At the same time, you have to remember to be prudent — that your clients are looking for high returns, not necessarily returns against the benchmark."

The mutual fund business is a competitive industry. Potential clients are always measuring to see how each fund is faring against the competitors in its peer group on both a short-term and long-term basis. In a market like technology that is moving all the time it is a challenge for portfolio managers to match a benchmark that can rise as fast as their portfolios, while at the same time keeping their eye on the future. They have to perform as well as the benchmark in the short term and beat it in the long term. Like any good investor, the good portfolio manager has to concentrate on the day-to-day rewards without losing out on the big wins.

We look for companies we think have the potential to continue to grow longer than people expect. If a company has good fundamentals and it suddenly gets whacked, that's a buying opportunity.

Ian Ainsworth, manager,
Altamira Science and Technology Fund

The Trimark Discovery Fund takes another approach. Its mandate is "to invest in innovative companies developing new products and services expected to produce exceptional growth in sales and earnings." While that doesn't exactly qualify for the technology sector list, to many people this mandate defines the sector. Trimark stipulates that though the Discovery Fund holdings will often be in the technology, telecommunications, biotechnology, or scientific fields, it also encompasses companies "revitalizing themselves through the technological spirit." Forty-five to 50 per cent of the companies in the Discovery Fund are in the information technology business, about 20 per cent are biotechnology, and the rest are growth companies in mature industries that are redefining themselves through the use of technology. "This is a volatile fund appealing to aggressive long-term investors prepared to make a long-term commitment in exchange for the potential of higher returns," says Discovery Fund portfolio manager Rick Serafini. "I'm bullish about the future of technology. It's a very detailed, high-touch type of investment that should be a percentage of everybody's portfolio."

How Mutual Funds Affect the Technology Stock Market

If you don't hold mutual funds, following their course can offer you an important insight into the market. *Investors Business Daily*, a US newspaper that's readily available, runs daily data about American mutual funds and their investments: how many funds own a particular stock, their largest investments, their top new buys, and their top sells. Institutional support indicates how solid the financial underpinning is for a company. Seeing where fund managers are parking their money and who is unloading what suggests a sense of the momentum. Several funds deciding to get out at the same time can create an incredible volatility, and a small investor can be caught in the crossfire.

The Grandaddy of Tech Funds

With assets under management approaching $4 billion, the T. Rowe Price Science and Technology Fund, based in Baltimore, is the number one technology fund and is within the top five of all mutual funds. The next biggest technology fund manages about $2.5 billion.

With a 10-year record, the T. Rowe Price Science and Technology Fund is one of the oldest technology funds. About 15 per cent of all the money invested in science and technology funds is

run by T. Rowe Price fund manager Chip Morris, a technology analyst since 1987 who has been running the fund since 1991. It
climbed a stellar 51.2 per cent in 1996, 28.3 per cent in 1994, and
in the past 10 years has returned 20.8 per cent. When he first
started with the fund, Morris remembers, the way to beat the market was to not have *anything* invested in the science and technology arena. Technology was a minefield in 1987. The two biggest
players in the sector, IBM and Digital, were careening downward.
IBM dropped from 160 to 50 and Digital from 202 to 18.

Chip Morris found the challenge he was looking for in this
sector. He discovered that technology is more fast paced and tax-
ing to keep up with than anything else he could have chosen. He
believed his skill to be his facility with figures. His dream job
entailed number crunching. Now he finds he reads like crazy.

I wanted something that changes all the time so that even in a
tough market I can find gems. The pace of change is so rapid
that you can spend 25 hours a day in researching companies
and picking investments.

Chip Morris, manager,
T. Rowe Price Science and Technology Fund

There are 80 stocks in the T. Rowe Price portfolio and the
core holdings keep changing. On average, two-thirds of the portfolio is invested in computer technology, reflecting Morris's bias
as a technology analyst. As well as three computer analysts, the
fund has two in health care, one in data services, and one in
telecommunications.

The fund tries to stay towards the leading edge by investing
in the most dynamic, most rapidly growing companies. The easy
way to manage, Chip Morris says, would be to pick the biggest

companies and while these always perform well, those aren't the most active companies. "In a tech fund, you always have to have a fresh portfolio," he says. "Newer is always better. Some of today's leaders will become tomorrow's laggers." The top 10 or 12 stocks in the portfolio contribute 30 to 35 per cent of the fund's assets, but it is the back end of the portfolio the analysts pay most attention to. "Before we had no tail," Chip Morris says. "With a tail, we are going to capture some of the newer, fresher ideas and it is going to serve us better over the longer term. If you recognize the names of those stocks, the story is probably over."

It takes a lot of time to stay on top. Selecting the best companies involves a lot of groundwork and travelling, going to trade shows, seminars, and visiting companies. The T. Rowe Price managers like to invest where they have what they call an information or insight advantage. That is why they prefer the smaller, less well-known companies. "The larger companies are well picked over by other analysts and the investor relations people are careful about the information they dispense," he says. "Anything you want to know, they can't tell you. Anything you don't care about, they are happy to waste your time letting you know all about."

The T. Rowe Price analysts like to meet with the technology company key executives, such as the head of R&D, the chief of sales, and the person running the service organization. As part of a large family of funds, with $90 billion of buying power representing all of T. Rowe Price's assets, this mass and scale makes most companies pretty accommodating with information. "Basically, we are always kicking tires," Morris says.

The research determines what the hot technology themes are and identifies which companies are participating in those themes. Like most technology watchers, Morris sees the Internet as the current theme, though he is more particular about the Internet niche he follows. He bases his decision on four selection criteria.

What Chip Morris is Looking for in the Internet

1. A sustainable business model with a propensity to deliver earnings;

2. A high level of intellectual property content, determined by high levels of both gross margin and share of market;

3. Companies embarking on strong product cycles;

4. Companies with management that has a strong vision and a proven ability to execute.

For the past six years, technology stocks have beaten the market soundly, so for technology managers and technology investors it has been uninterrupted bliss. Everybody says a correction is just around the corner but Chip Morris asks, "Where is that corner?" Though 7 or 8 per cent of its assets are in cash, Morris considers the fund to be fully invested. He wants that amount of cushion so that if the market does correct, there is enough cash flow to go out and buy stocks at a much lower price.

If there is indeed a correction, he thinks it could be quite a fierce one. "We never try to time the market. We invest in health care, data services, and telecommunications so that if there is a severe correction, we can take money back from the other segments and restock the computer-based segment," Morris says. He thinks the market can correct as much as 10 or 15 per cent, but he sees it as a buying opportunity, not Disaster City.

"Technology is like playing Russian roulette with all six chambers loaded," he says. The proper approach he feels is to look for aggressive growth while accepting that there is a risk of loss. He invests in stocks with an 18- to 36-month horizon, but he expects his investors to stick with him for three to five years. "Certainly it's not for the conservative investor who wants a dividend yield or access to the money in a hurry. The longer your horizon, the more appropriate this vehicle is for you."

Chip Morris sees technology as a great sector for dollar-cost averaging — investing on a regular basis no matter what the market is doing. Dollar-cost averaging forces the discipline to buy low and buy less when the market is high. "People tend to invest with their gut and their gut tells them to buy when things are looking great and to sell when things look like they are going into the tank. You should really do the opposite," he says.

With a mutual fund you get one person making decisions for many. In the next chapter we'll find how many people can make decisions as one.

```
45...DEG↑365...RKDE↓85...SCEB↑22.34...ITS↓956
```

CANADIAN TECHNOLOGY MUTUAL FUNDS LISTED IN DESCENDING ORDER OF ASSETS UNDER MANAGEMENT AS OF DECEMBER 1997

Royal Life Science and Technology Fund
Green Line Science and Technology Fund
Mackenzie Universal World Science and Technology Fund
CIBC Global Technology Fund
Altamira Science and Technology Fund
First Canadian Global Science and Technology Fund
C I Global Technology Sector Fund
AIM Global Technology Fund
Fidelity Focus Technology Fund
Talvest/Hyperion Global Science and Technology Fund
Canadian Science and Technology Growth Fund
First Trust North American Technology Trust 97
Middlefield Global Technology Fund
Hartford Canadian Advanced Technology Fund
Navigator Canadian Technology Fund

`45...DEG↑365...RKDE↓85...SCEB↑22.34...ITS↓956`

US TECHNOLOGY SECTOR MUTUAL FUNDS

Name	Symbol
Fidelity Select Electronics	FSELX
Seligman Communications&Information A	SLMCX
Seligman Communications&Information B	SLMBX
Seligman Communications&Information D	SLMDX
Fidelity Select Computers	FDCPX
Fidelity Advisor Technology Instl	
Fidelity Advisor Technology A	
Fidelity Advisor Technology T	FATEX
Seligman Henderson Glob Technology A	SHGTX
Principal Preserv PSE Tech 100 Index	PPTIX
Seligman Henderson Glob Technology D	SHTDX
Seligman Henderson Glob Technology B	SHTBX
Fidelity Select Technology	FSPTX
Merrill Lynch Technology A	MATCX
Merrill Lynch Technology D	MDTCX
Northern Technology	NTCHX
Merrill Lynch Technology B	MBTCX
Merrill Lynch Technology C	MCTCX
RCM Global Technology	
Interactive Investments Tech Value	TVFQX
Franklin DynaTech I	FKDNX
Robertson Stephens Information Age A	RSIFX
PBHG Technology & Communications	PBTCX
Franklin DynaTech II	
Alliance Technology Adv	ATEYX
John Hancock Global Technology A	NTTFX
John Hancock Global Technology B	FGTBX
Alliance Technology A	ALTFX
Ivy Global Science & Technology A	IVTA
Kemper Technology A	KTCAX
Alliance Technology C	ATECX
Alliance Technology B	ATEBX
Fidelity Select Software & Comp	FSCSX
Ivy Global Science & Technology B	

45...DEG↑365...RKDE↓85...SCEB↑22.34...ITS↓956

US TECHNOLOGY SECTOR MUTUAL FUNDS

Name	Symbol
Ivy Global Science & Technology C	
Kemper Technology B	KTCBX
Kemper Technology C	KTCCX
Invesco Strategic Technology	FTCHX
PIMCo Innovation A	PIVAX
PIMCo Innovation C	PIVCX
PIMCo Innovation B	PIVBX
EV Traditional Information Age	ETIAX
EV Marathon Information Age	EMIAX
First American Technology C	FATCX
First American Technology A	FATAX
First American Technology B	FITBX
T. Rowe Price Science & Technology	PRSCX
Monterey Murphy New World Tech Conv	MNWCX
United Science & Technology A	UNSCX
Amerindo Technology D	ATCHX
Icon Technology	CTEX

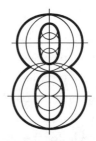

INVESTMENT CLUBS: GETTING IT ALL TOGETHER

The Team Approach

Ten heads are better than one. An investment club shares the work that has to go into being a successful investor. Each member should be willing to spend at least four or five hours a month reading the financial papers and watching the business news on television. On a regular basis, each member should present a report to the group outlining a company's business, management, price history, sales, earnings, and potential. A member who contributes money and nothing else is not a valuable participant.

While investment clubs are a good way for beginners to get their feet wet as investors, many seasoned investors use them as a way to maximize their long-term profits and to expand their information base. Because most clubs invest for growth, members are less likely to panic when the market drops or interest rates change. The membership has to vote as a group on what to buy and sell, making it harder to fall in love with a stock and never take a profit on it.

The rigours of a club oblige the investor to comply with the accepted principles of successful investing because it encourages dollar-cost-averaging, the strategy of investing at regular intervals regardless of the short-term market outlook; promotes diversification, balancing growth with income and small cap with large cap; and precludes market timing, trying to guess the cycles of the market. Also, peripherally, by buying larger lots of shares, the club saves on broker commissions.

The members of the club should share a coherent investment philosophy. If some members are risk averse and want solid dividends and long-term capital growth, while others want to buy small-cap start-ups, there could be problems. It is worth spending time developing a uniformity of style and purpose and writing workable rules that everybody in the group can agree on.

The investment strategies for investment clubs do not differ drastically from those of individual investors. But an investment club is a team. It is up to each player to contribute equally. If one wins, all win. If one loses....

The Basics

With close to 3000 in North America, investment clubs are becoming increasingly popular as ways for ordinary people to pool their money and become stock market players. The pooling of resources and expertise allows for more leverage in the market place. One doesn't have to be a Bay Street or Wall Street stockbroker to be successful at playing the market, and some investment clubs have had more success than professional managers.

The model the Victoria Investment Club has chosen for picking stocks is to have individual members research and make presentations on their picks, after which the group debates their potential. Of course, trust is an extremely important aspect of any investment club, and members have to believe in each other's stock picks and judgement or they will never reach a consensus on what to buy.

Individuals within the group focusing on particular stocks ensures there has been a thorough study of potential investments. Research is done through the traditional methods of reading newspapers and specialized investment publications, watching business shows, talking to brokers, and using the Internet and stock-investing software programs.

Tips for Technology Investment Clubs

The National Association of Investors Corp. (NAIC) is a US-based non-profit education group that represents clubs and individual investors. These tips for technology investors is based on their advice to investment clubs:

1. **Invest regularly.** Agree on an amount that each member is expected to contribute to the club on a monthly basis. Even a small amount to get started can show you what the possibilities are.

2. **Don't try to time the market.** Keep the money in stocks all the time. Do not increase or decrease the stockholdings based on the outlook for the market or the economy. By staying fully invested, the club will never have to worry about missing a big rally.

3. **Rely on research, not good stories.** Chasing stocks based on a good story can result in a serious loss for all involved. Sure, a good story may result in a big gain occasionally, but nothing beats good research.

4. **Buy solid stocks and hang on to them.** Make a commitment to a stock and stay with it, even when the market is slow. It hurts to act too quickly, especially in technology stocks, which can rise and fall drastically in short spans of time, so be patient and ride the waves. Longevity is the key.

5. **Review your portfolio regularly.** The previous tip does not mean never sell. The tricky thing in growth-stock investing

is knowing when to sell. Since selling is emotional as well as analytic, this can be a dilemma for a club, possibly even harder than deciding to buy the stock in the first place.

6. **Balance the risk within your portfolio.** You've heard this one before. Diversifying your portfolio over small and large companies, and throughout industries, ensures limited risk.

How to Start Your Own Club

1. **Keep membership to a manageable number.** If the club has too many members, it may be difficult to come to a consensus on any decision. If the club has too few members, it may be difficult to accumulate the funds and expertise necessary to build a portfolio that can achieve substantial returns. The core in the Victoria Investment Club is 10 people. Not everybody comes all the time.

2. **Keep contributions reasonable.** The club should be able to make regular stock purchases without straining members' finances. No amount is too small or too large as long as everybody can afford it. If any members feel that it is not enough, they are still free to invest on their own outside the club.

3. **Make sure everyone is prepared to participate.** An investment club is a team in which all members must contribute. It is not a fund you put your money in for someone else to manage. Everyone is in it together, and it is each member's responsibility to research and recommend stocks that the club should invest in.

4. **Make sure everyone has similar goals.** This needs to be clearly established at the first meeting. Issues such as the amount of contribution, the risk level you are willing to accept, and the time commitment expected from each member need to be agreed upon from the get-go.

5. **Get legal help**. For legal purposes, clubs should be registered as a business, usually a partnership, in which each member can be taxed individually.

The Victoria Investment Club

The Victoria Investment Club invests solely in technology. The members meet on a regular basis, in our case every two weeks, to discuss ideas and to collaborate on investing. They all bring some expertise about investing in technology to the club from their backgrounds as computer scientists, consultants, technology journalists, marketers, and serious technology investors.

Theoretically, the interchange between the members should allow for everybody to offer his or her opinion and agree on the most astute investments. The reality is that the club is often stymied by the accumulation of knowledge which highlights the amount of risk in these investments. Here are the minutes of a Victoria Investment Club meeting from the summer of 1997 which demonstrates how decisions are made, or not made:

The Club Minutes

1. We discussed investment philosophy. We are most interested in junior companies that already have some weight and small companies with emerging technologies. There is a consensus that the group would like to develop a diversified portfolio of large- and small-cap stocks with the emphasis on "not quite first-class companies with strong relations to first-class companies." Our philosophy is to be medium-term holders, not flippers of stocks.

2. Edward suggested that we consider Image Processing Systems Inc. — (IPV.TSE) 52-week high $2.70, low $1.40, Monday's close $2.50 (up nine cents on the day on volume of 161,000

shares) — as our first investment. Image Processing Systems is a new company, listed for about two months, involved in the digital testing of computer and TV monitors and the inspection of beer bottles. It has contracts with many of the major TV and computer monitor manufacturers, and revenue for the first six months of the year was $5.2 million, a fivefold increase over the corresponding period a year earlier. It is just entering digital testing of bottles, as a potentially lucrative second product. The stock is averaging around $2.35.

Andrew, Edward, and Dave checked them out. Andrew contacted various investment houses to see if they had research on company. He discovered analysts are predicting $5 within 18 months. Is that too long a horizon for us? They also warn that the company success is very dependent on two of its senior managers. Edward contacted the investors relations department and passed out some information they provided, including the annual report. He said we could arrange to tour the Scarborough plant.

Dave summarized the latest published information about Image Processing Systems: Image Processing Systems stock is edging higher as it announces a new deal in Asia. The Toronto-based company said it has received an order worth more than $4.9-million for 23 of its automated display inspection systems from LG Electronics of South Korea. LG is going to use Image's systems to inspect and align picture tubes for computer monitors. Image Processing say the deal "creates a window for additional orders from plants around the world." As of April 7, the company had more than $9 million worth of orders on the book.

3. Discussion about Gandalf. The Club had discussed Gandalf at the previous meeting, and four days later it tripled in value. The next day, it lost all its increased value. The stock is now trading at $2.50, about two and a half times what it was when it first came up for discussion.

Conclusion: Gandalf is unpredictable because the movement has nothing to do with the fundamentals of the company. Its patents are losing value. Its assets are knowledgable people supporting a bad product. The unknowns are its technology and whether or not there is a takeover bid on the table. Not a buy. (Soon after these minutes were transcribed in the summer of 1997, Gandalf went bankrupt.)

4. Metronet. A new company which is poised to enter the local telephone market when it is deregulated. The company does not trade publicly but is ripe for a public offering. Let's get in early. Andrew was to investigate. He has since found out that Metronet is looking for investment from strategic partners. The amount of investment the company is seeking as a private equity investment is far beyond our reach. (Metronet went public in December 1997 at $23 a share under the symbol MNC on the Toronto Stock Exchange and with the symbol METNF on NASDAQ.)

5. Sun Microsystems (SUNW. NASDAQ). Sun has 40 per cent of the workstation market and is achieving some success breaking out of the academic and engineering niche into the financial sector. It is shifting into high-end servers, where the margins are better than they are for more competitive workstations. Ken says Sun seems to be a preferred employer for people with technical expertise. Still not clear how they will make money out of Java. In 1986 Sun was trading at $16. The stock has split four times and is now trading at $35 with a P/E of 20. Ken is to look at the value of Sun in relation to HP, Digital, and IBM, its most direct competitors.

6. During a discussion about the two-way radio market in Asia, where it is too expensive to establish cellular networks, Ericsson (ERICY.NASDAQ) was raised as a possible candidate because 20 to 30 per cent of its market is in two-way radios in Asia. Ken

has an interest in this area and we will ask for his comments. Jerome to find out fundamentals. Dave to get annual report.

Conclusion: It was felt that since Ericsson, which was discussed at the previous meeting, was trading near its historic high, it was not a suitable candidate at this time.

7. Low orbiting satellites: Qualcomm, Motorola, TRW, and Raytheon were discussed. (Qualcomm signed a major deal this week, and there seems to be a buzz about this company.) There have been some recent large contracts. It was resolved to find out more on the Internet, by calling the company, and networking.

8. CAE — high-end flight simulators. There are only two or three airline manufacturers so there are only two or three possible customers. Dave to research status of customer relations.

9. First Class Systems (FCS.VSE) on-line educational software. The company has received grants from the New Brunswick government. Resolved to look at public money and grants and how companies that might be affected by them.

10. Discussion about Direct TV, Tee-Com's problems, and the impact it will have on ExpressVu getting a licence. No resolution.

11. Discussion about Advantax (ADX.TSE). Arrangement with Visa to offer a seamless 20 per cent discount off purchases. No resolution.

12. It was felt that Hewlett-Packard had unfairly taken a hit and was a possibility as a buying opportunity.

13. It was decided to get information on BCI, the international unit BCE is spinning off. David suggested we should do some "structural filtering" of prospective stocks by, for example, examining a list of 25 telecom companies.

The Victoria Investment Club to meet again two weeks from Tuesday.

Part 2

Disclosing the Enigma: The Technology Segments Uncovered

Part 1 of *The Secrets of Investing in Technology Stocks* gave you the tools and strategies for understanding the investment theories and philosophies that would help you prosper in the hot technology stock market. Part 2 will offer an in-depth look at some of the segments that make up the field of opportunities and dreams or, if you aren't careful, nightmares.

The 1100 companies, more or less, that make up the technology sector hardly ever move in lock step. What the semiconductor, software, hardware, telecommunications, and biotechnology segments do have in common is that they employ the most advanced science, usually digital, and they are growing incredibly quickly. While you don't have to understand the minute details of the science, this section will give you an insider's look at each segment and how to approach it as an investor. You will get a feel for what makes each segment attractive, and what to beware of.

For most of the segments, there is a list of companies that form the group. This is by no means an exhaustive list, since the terrain changes too quickly, and there is much overlap. It is more an opportunity to learn some of the names and perhaps a chance to do some comparisons and screening of companies that compete directly. Part 1 gave you the binoculars to scan the technology field; this section gives you the microscope to hone right in for your own close examination without the intrusion of a view from above. By the time you could follow a specific buy or sell recommendation, it would be too late anyway.

The companies are listed in order of size, with the most highly capitalized first, down to the smallest cap. Not surprisingly, Microsoft is at the top of many of the lists. Next to the name of the company is its ticker symbol. If a company has four letters or more in its symbol, it probably trades on NASDAQ, and if it has three letters or less, it probably trades on the New York Stock Exchange, but you can't assume anything with technology stocks.

SEMICONDUCTORS AND MICROPROCESSORS

We believe the semiconductor industry will not fully mature for
another 20 years or so.

Marleau Lemire Securities Inc.,
Canadian High Tech Industry Review 1997

The semiconductor, the steam engine of our era, is an electronic system or integrated circuit of transistors and resistors built
into a single microchip of silicon crystal or other material. It
contains the arithmetic, logic, and control circuitry required to
interpret and execute instructions from a computer program and
it is the brains of any computer or computing device. Developed
during the 1970s, the microprocessor lowered the size, weight,
and cost of electronic components, leading to inexpensive consumer appliances and electronic devices. This in turn made possible the personal computer. In 1968, there were only 30,000
computers in the world. But in 1996 alone, over 70 million PCs
were sold around the world.

At last estimate, the semiconductor industry was worth over
$150 billion and is growing at a rate of about 40 per cent a year.

In 1995, Intel alone had revenues of $20.8 billion, with earning per share up 44 per cent. Since 1978, the semiconductor industry has had only one year of negative revenue growth — in 1985 — and this followed a year in which revenues grew 45 per cent.

The Intel Story

The influence of Intel is so pervasive that many people think it is the only chip manufacturer. Founded in 1968 with capital of less than $5 million, it now owns 75 per cent of the microprocessor market and, though it has had its ups and downs over the years, its earnings are growing at an average rate of 37 per cent a year. To maintain its supremacy over time, it has spent over $10 billion on research and development and to expand its production capacity. *The Wall Street Journal* predicts Intel could become the most profitable company in the world.

In 1968, two engineers, Gordon Moore and Robert Noyce, resigned from Fairchild Semiconductor, the first company to work exclusively in silicon and which pioneered the use of silicon in electronics. Earlier they were part of "The Traitorous Eight," a larger group of engineers who in 1957 had left Shockley Labs, where they had worked with William Shockley, the co-inventor of the transistor. Armed solely with the track records of the two partners and the following one-page business plan Robert Noyce typed up himself — typos and all — in less than two days, venture capitalist Arthur Rock was able to line up the $2.5 million in cash they needed from investors in order to finance their startup.

Based on this business plan, how many people would have been prepared to risk their capital? Twenty people did. And they are still benefiting.

With its market dominance and its financial muscle, Intel is clearly the colossus, but there are competitors in this industry worth looking at. Open a circuit board and you will find chips

Intel's Original Business Plan *

The company will engage in research, development, and manufacture and sales of integrated electronic structures to fulfill the needs of electronic systems manufacturers. This will include thin films, thick films, semiconductor devices, and other solid state components used in hybrid and monolithic integrated structures.

A variety of processes will be established, both at a laboratory and production level. These include crystal growth, slicing, lapping, polishing, solid state diffusion, photolithographic masking and etching, vacuum evaporation, film deposition, assembly, packaging, and testing, as well as the development and manufacture of special processing and testing equipment required to carry out these processes.

Products may include diodes, transistors, field effect devices, photo sensitive devices, photo emitting devices, integrated circuits, and subsystems commonly referred to by the phrase "large scale integration." Principal customers for these products are expected to be the manufacturers of advanced electronic systems for communications, radar, control and data processing. It is anticipated that many of these customers mill be located outside California.

The original plan as typed by Robert Noyce, including the typos.

named NEC, Hyundai, Goldstar, Hitachi, TXC, and, of course, Motorola. While Intel's success is driven by the personal computer, semiconductors drive consumer electronics, telecommunications, automobiles, and are even part of children's toys, identification cards, and traffic lights.

The 30-year-old Intel is a splendidly run, progressive company that is constantly reinventing itself. Its product cycles are becoming shorter and shorter, with constant demand for the latest and the fastest. Its "Intel Inside" marketing campaign has given it a cachet and brand-name appeal that rivals Coca-Cola and Cadillac.

While Intel is technically a semiconductor company, unlike other chip makers, its business is so tightly focused on the PC market that the issues for investors are all computer-oriented. The price cycles and price performance of computer hardware affects Intel's stock performance. How quickly and enthusiastically software manufacturers adapt to the latest chip Intel brings to market are the factors that move its share price up and down.

"Investors ask us a lot of questions about computer strategy and products and how they interrelate with our business," says Gordon Casey, Intel's director of investor relations. "In our industry, software and standards issues are what affect the investment decisions."

More than half of Intel's stock is held by institutions all over the world. With their short-term focus, they are always emphasizing the current quarter's earnings. However, the analysts who make stock recommendations to individual investors put more emphasis on the long term. "The least little thing we say can have a tremendous impact on the stock, even if they are little comments the man on the street might think are trivial," says Casey.

Intel's Pentium chip crisis, when a flaw in the chip's design caused minor calculation errors, threatened to undermine trust in the reliability of PCs and confidence in the company itself. Intel turned the crisis into a triumphant promotion of its Pentium brand. After a shaky start when it tried to downplay the impact of the bug, Intel used the opportunity to promote its reliability and to highlight its brand through an aggressive advertising campaign. A recent market survey showed that corporate computer buyers were willing to pay at least $350 more for a PC with an Intel chip than for a computer without one.

Semiconductor Opportunities

In a process known in the technology trade as migration to the microprocessor, operations that used to be programmed into hardware and software are now being engineered right into the chips, so that the semiconductors are becoming more powerful. So much of the technology is in the chip that many computer manufacturers have in some ways simply become low-cost pack-agers for the semiconductor companies. The computers are becoming commodity items, hard to differentiate from each other, while Intel sets the pace of innovation. Many computer manufacturers are trying to defend themselves from domination by this powerful supplier by developing their own chips, with mixed success.

The challenge for the chip manufacturers is the escalating cost of manufacturing. It costs more than $1 billion to build a typical fabrication plant. Many have heard Moore's Law, coined by Gordon Moore, formerly chairman of Intel, which says the number of transistors that can be packed on a chip doubles about every 18 months. Fewer people have heard the corollary, Rock's Law, coined by Intel director Arthur Rock, which states that the cost of the equipment and facilities to manufacture these semi-conductors doubles every four years.

In the commodity part of the semiconductor business, there is high investment interest in companies that are well capitalized and that have the ability to produce a differentiated product at a reasonable cost. One way investors could play on the growth of the overall industry is by buying shares of Applied Materials, the premier manufacturer of chipmaking equipment such as wafer fabrication systems and sensitive devices that layer chips with electrical circuits. Chipmaking equipment itself is expected to be an $80-billion-a-year industry by 2000.

Because of the intense competition, the semiconductor segment is volatile in the extreme. Because of this volatility, the semiconductor segment has been referred to as "risk on steroids." When customers buying decisions were based on price and reliable delivery, the industry tended to swing from scarcity to overcapacity, leading to extreme boom and bust cycles. But with more attention to niche products, the semiconductor segment is less risky than in the early days, when products were interchangeable. The one exception is memory chips, which are becoming more of a commodity. Wall Street fears that a recent slowdown in the market for memory chips would somehow signal a cyclical bust for the whole semiconductor industry, indeed for all technology, are so far unfounded.

"Commodity trading is a different kind of investing," says Hambrecht & Quist senior analyst Doug van Dorsten. "You want to own the stock at a point in time when the commodity is scarce and the demand for it is rising. But in many cases, you want to buy the commodity during a time of adjustment and correction when demand is falling and there is excess supply."

However, Intel's Gordon Casey doesn't think that memory chips are a reflection of the health of the semiconductor segment. "Semiconductor technology brings so much value to the market place," he says. "Fortunately, we aren't in a mature industry where we are bringing about small improvements. We are bringing huge improvements, so growth is going to continue for quite a while."

The Intel Story: A Scenario

Intel success is based on the fact that they keep coming out with new products that cannibalize their old products, and that way they stay ahead of their competition. But most people in technology are not that fortunate and have a lot of competition. They may be the leader today but may not the leader a year from today.

Edward Jamieson, portfolio manager, Franklin Resources Inc.

Semiconductor Groups

45...DEG↑365...RKDE↓85...SCEB↑22.34...ITS↓956

BROAD PRODUCT LINE: THE BIG GUYS

Company	Ticker Symbol
Intel	INTC
Motorola	MOT
Texas Instruments	TXN
National Semiconductor	NSM
Advanced Micro Devices	AMD
Cypress Semiconductor	CY
Cirrus Logic	CRU
Integrated Device Technology	IDTI

`45...DEG↑365...RKDE↓85...SCEB↑22.34...ITS↓956`

EQUIPMENT/MATERIALS MANUFACTURERS

Company name	Ticker Symbol
Applied Materials	AMAT
KLA Instrument	KLAC
Teradyne	TER
Novellus Systems	NVLS
Lam Research	LRCX
Etec System	ETEC
Silicon Valley Group	SVGI
MEMC Electronic Materials	WFR
Dupont Photomasks	DPMI
PRI Automation	PRIA
Kulicke & Soffa Industries	KLIC
Credence Systems	CMOS
Cymer	CYMI
Ultratech Stepper	UTEK
Photronics	PLAB
SpeedFam	SFAM
Helix Technology	HELX
Integrated Process Equipment	IPEC
Electroglas	EGLS
FSI International	FSII
Veeco Instruments	VECO
Cohu	COHU
Asyst Technologies	ASYT
Cree Research	CREE
Advanced Technology Materials	ATMID
Watkins-Johnson	WJ
ADE	ADEX
LTX	LTXX
Gasonics	GSNX
Semitool	SMTL
Brooks Automation	BRKS
Aetrium	ATRM
CFM Technologies	CFMT
Mattson Technology	MTSN

`45...DEG↑365...RKDE↓85...SCEB↑22.34...ITS↓956`

Emcore	EMKR
Reliability	REAL
Integrated Measurement Systems	IMSC
Nanometrics	NANO
Micrion	MICN
Genus	GGNS
Tegal	TGAL
IBIS Technology	IBIS
Submicron Systems	SUBM
Aseco	ASEC
Photon Dynamics	PHTN
Trikon Technologies	TRKN

MEMORY MAKERS

Company name	Ticker Symbol
Intel	INTC
Motorola	MOT
Texas Instruments	TXN
Micron Technology	MU
National Semiconductor	NSM
Advanced Micro Devices	AMD
Atmel	ATML
Smart Modular Technologies	SMOD
Cypress Semiconductor	CY
Rambus	RMBS
Integrated Device Technology	IDTI
SanDisk	SNDK
Alliance	ALSC
Ramtron	RMTR
Integrated Silicon Solutions	ISSI
Silicon Storage Technology	SSTI
Xicor	XICO
Dense-Pac Microsystems	DPAC
Catalyst Semiconductor	CATS

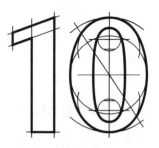

COMPUTERS AND HARDWARE

The PC is not a particularly interesting device; they don't represent a particularly great use of technology. They are just a clumsy way to connect to the Internet right now. Microsoft owns all the applications categories and they have no real interest in doing much innovation, so the whole PC space is just kind of boring.

William Joy, vice-president of research, Sun Microsystems

Basically, they all look the same. Without a nameplate, it is hard to differentiate between an IBM, Compaq, or Dell computer. Most of them sport "Intel Inside" labels so that even under the hood performance is similar. The way to tell them apart is through brand recognition, speed to market with innovations, distribution and marketing, and the words that make every investor shudder, price competition.

Because of competition, the hardware businesses, or what some in the business call the execution businesses, have low profit margins. Besides computers, other execution businesses are disk drives, circuit boards, printers, and peripherals. Despite the low profit margins, according to Seligman Communications and Information Fund manager Paul Wick, these types of businesses can be fantastic investments.

The Franchise

The key thing is to find companies that have established what Paul Wick calls a franchise. A franchise is a company with strong customer loyalty, or a company so well managed that it can maintain its edge, even in a commodity market. "Franchises don't die overnight," Mr. Wick says, "and the individual investor has plenty of time to figure out if the franchise has gone bad."

Dell Computer and Gateway 2000 are both examples of franchises. With their direct sales model, they have both been able to establish strong brand names — Gateway with the residential consumer, Dell with the small-business customer. Both are extremely well managed, and even with net profit margins at only 5 or 6 per cent, returns on equity and cash flow for both companies is high. Dell had revenues of $9.8 billion for the last four quarters with a recent return of invested capital of 167 per cent, the highest return of any major computer systems company. Gateway 2000, founded in September 1985, by 1996 had recorded annual net sales of $5.04 billion.

Some people are very short-sighted and bigoted in the way they look at technology companies. Even some professional investors only invest in networking and software companies, and end up missing a lot of great investment opportunities in hardware because they have blinders on.

Paul Wick, manager,
Seligman Communications and Information Fund

The Dell Example

Dell, the world's leading direct marketer of computer systems, is the perfect example of a technology that was made by marketing. It doesn't spend enough on research and development to truly be considered a technology company, but it did invent something that makes it stand out — its sales and distribution network. The direct sales model has kept Dell fashionable with both computer consumers and with the stock market. With a 206 per cent return in 1996, and 270 per cent in 1997 to date, the stock price performance is way beyond what one would expect based on sheer earnings.

"With a direct model, we gain huge leverage opportunities," says Frank Milano of Dell's investor relations group. "Compaq, for instance, has no knowledge of who buys their PCs because they sell them through an intermediary like CompUSA or Best Buy." With the steady upward slope, some investors felt they might have missed a buying opportunity, and the Dell investor relations office telephone kept ringing steadily. "If you thought the momentum was over last year, you missed a strong ride," Milano would tell the callers.

Typical technology investors, the Dell callers are risk takers prepared to weather the vagaries of the market who are investing outside their RRSPs, their 401K, or IRA accounts. "You have to have a steel stomach for the daily churning that goes on in our market space," Frank Milano says. With no dividend program to explain, the inquiries he fields are about growth opportunities facing the company as well as growth opportunities facing the industry. "We get the heat-seeking crowd," Milano says.

Frank Milano's Advice

1. **Keep an eye on 10 years out**. Though the sector is volatile in the short term, it is the long-term strategy that is going to determine the success of the investment.

2. **Look worldwide**. National brands, like Siemens in Germany and Olivetti in Italy, are strong enough in their domestic markets that they are in the top 10 worldwide. But they still have little market share outside their home country.

3. **Look for consolidation**. The opportunities in hardware investing will come about because even the biggest players have less than 10 per cent market share globally, and they are going to look for mergers and acquisitions to penetrate foreign markets. One example of consolidation was the agreement between NEC, the largest computer manufacturer in Japan, and the American leader, Packard Bell. "In terms of consolidation, you have to say the industry is in its infancy," Frank Milano says. "The US is closest to maturity."

4. **Look for bobbers in the water**. What companies are rising to the top in a fluid environment?

5. **Follow what Intel is doing**. "We are servants to the technology transitions that the chipmakers, Intel primarily, bring to the box," says Frank Milano. "Their chips are constantly fuelling new life cycles and causing a generational effect."

Technology has to be represented in a model portfolio. But the advice most investors hear from careful investors like Peter Lynch is to buy what they know and understand. The problem is that technology can be so complex that awareness and comprehension can really limit the array of choice. For some people, the computer sitting on their desktop is the only piece of technology they recognize. So if the computer on your desk is what you know, why ignore it?

Does Your Hardware Company Investment Measure Up?

1. Is it perceived in the market place as a technology leader?

2. What is its rate of growth?

3. Does it have a proven performance record in the market place?

4. Does its brand identity have value?

5. Has it established a brand identity outside its home country?

6. Is it quick to take advantage of technology changes?

7. What software, Internet, and telecommunications partners does it have?

8. Is its management qualified?

9. Are its distribution channels innovative?

10. Is it taking advantage of volume purchases?

Big Computers and Little Computers

The computer world doesn't end at the desktop. Companies still use mainframes and workstations for enterprise-wide functions like human resource tracking and accounting. Mission-critical applications like credit card billing and airline reservation, where mistakes are costly and crashes are deadly, still need the power and reliability of the mainframe. So hardware companies like IBM, Digital Equipment Corporation, and Sun Microsystems making big computers continue to be viable investments, and so do the software companies creating programs for big companies, as we will see in the next chapter.

The most ballyhooed new computing device coming down the pike is the $500 network computer. These Internet-oriented computers without operating systems are being enthusiastically embraced by Oracle Systems, Sun Microsystems, and IBM in their struggle against the Microsoft hegemony. Some analysts predict NC computers will be the hot gift items of the decade, and the boom in NCs could be bigger than it was for PCs in the early eighties. Of course, Microsoft, with its business vested in the Windows operating systems, thinks of them as a passing fancy and is countering with its Windows NT operating system and its Internet strategy. One research study projects only 7 million NCs selling by the year 2000, compared with an estimated 100 million units of PCs shipped during the same time. The middle-of-the-road camp says consumers will buy an NC in addition to a PC with most high-end users continuing to use their full-featured PCs to write reports, do research on the Internet, and access other server applications, while the NC is relegated to data entry functions. That way everybody wins and personal computers will not be going the way of the typewriter.

Those bearish about the hardware segment describe the computer as merely a bunch of electronic components banged into a box. Compared to software, these pessimists see the hardware segment as beset with high capital costs, slow rates of growth, and, by definition, larger, more bureaucratic organizations. Over time, they say, the box makers will slash profit margins and battle over who can build the box most cheaply. Computers will cease being a growth investment.

The Bleak View

I see a huge shakeout in the PC market, just like the TV industry. There used to be a zillion manufacturers, but today there are only a few. I predict a gloomy future for PC makers like AST Research, Apple Computer, and privately held Packard Bell. IBM and Digital Equipment Corp. will also be hard-pressed to maintain viable PC businesses. Probable long-term winners? Compaq Computer, Hewlett-Packard, Dell Computer, and Gateway 2000.

John Maxwell, managing director,
SoundView Financial Group in Stamford, Connecticut

45...DEG↑365...RKDE↓85...SCEB↑22.34...ITS↓956

A PC IN EVERY HOME: SMALL BUSINESS COMPUTER COMPANIES

Company	Ticker Symbol
IBM	IBM
Hewlett-Packard	HWP
Compaq	CPQ
Dell	DELL
Digital Equipment	DEC
Gateway 2000	GTW
Apple Computer	AAPL
Micron Electronics	MUEI
Vitech America	VTCH
The Panda Project	PNDA

45...DEG↑365...RKDE↓85...SCEB↑22.34...ITS↓956

SERVERS AND WORKSTATIONS: THE COMPUTER WORKHORSES

Company	Ticker Symbol
IBM	IBM
Hewlett-Packard	HWP
Compaq	CPQ
Dell	DELL
Sun Microsystems	SUNW
Digital Equipment	DEC
NCR	NCR
Unisys	UIS
Silicon Graphics	SGI
Network Appliance	NTAP
Data General	DGN
Sequent	SQNT
Stratus Computer	SRA
Auspex	ASPX
The Panda Project	PNDA
Texas Micro	TEXM

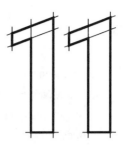

SOFTWARE: THE MICROSOFT UNIVERSE

> Why do you invest in stocks? You invest for growth — you discount for risk, and it's fair to say that it's difficult to find a business that can demonstrate cash flow growth faster than software.
>
> *Douglas van Dorsten,*
> *senior technology analyst, Hambrecht & Quist*

Microsoft became the second most valuable company in the world in the summer of 1997 as its shares rose by $10 in one day to close at $150 US. The stock, up 80 per cent since December 1996, would have been trading at close to $300 if it hadn't split two for one six months earlier. With a market capitalization of $177.9 billion, it surged ahead of Coca-Cola and was behind only General Electric Company.

A Microsoft Strategy

One of the first questions you have to ask about a software company is what is their Microsoft strategy? If the answer is what do you mean, you run the other way. They have to have a Microsoft strategy.

Rick Serafini, manager, Trimark Discovery Fund

Microsoft is the final word in investing in the software segment. It's the benchmark against which every other software company measures its current or anticipated success. It's the song of lamentation defunct software companies sing after they have succumbed to its power. A relationship with Microsoft is the badge of achievement every aspiring software start-up boasts as its ticket to success. It is also the mantle of fear the severing of those relations will mean. The first question any investor in a new software opportunity asks is: Can it run under the Microsoft Windows operating system and interface? The next question is: Will Microsoft covet the product and kill the company to get it?

In real estate investing, the mantra is location, location, location. In software, it is timing, timing, timing. Just like comedy, timing is everything. Software companies, especially new ones, soar and then often sink. The trick for investors is to get in early and get out before it's too late. Software companies thrive when there is a new and unique product that everybody needs — an Internet browser or a personal information manager, for instance. If the company gets the product to market quickly and resolutely enough, their business will thrive. But as soon as the rest of the market catches up, it can sink with a thud. That's why many astute investors consider software as a short-term buy, viable until the competition attacks with a new product.

Watch Your Back

Software is relatively easy to duplicate. There is patent protection, but in many cases companies don't rely on patents because they know there are ways around patents.

Robert McWhirter, vice-president and portfolio manager,
Royal Bank Investment Management

A software company is obliged to constantly create the forced obsolescence of its own products. If it doesn't, Microsoft will, or another new company will come along and try to capture the market. The gobble-me-up nature of software is constant upgrades and changes. However, software companies have an installed legacy to support, and its products have to be backward compatible. The remains of WordStar, Borland Visual dBASE, and Lotus 1-2-3 attest to this precarious predicament.

The software sector is quite broad and how you would evaluate Microsoft Corporation, Adobe Systems Incorporated, Symantec Corporation, or McAfee Associates Inc. compared to a small start-up stock is pretty different. Typically a start-up stock can command fabulous price to earnings ratios because the valuation is based on growth rates and revenue recognition. Investors look for companies that can maintain their position for as long as possible when the crunch comes. Marketing, advertising, merchandising, and good lawyers can help them hold on until they invent the next product.

In most cases, investors can toss the traditional price to earnings valuation out the window. The reason to invest in software is to profit from the incredible growth potential these companies have. Getting in early means getting in before earnings start flooding in, and because these companies have very little earnings, software investors have to look at price to revenues, and even more importantly, growth of revenues rather than P/E ratios. Growth and revenue is what drives stock value in the software sector. Investors put a lot of weight on quarter-to-quarter results. "I think that that's a mindless way to invest," says Lori Barker, manager of investor relations and competitive analysis for Symantec Corporation. "When I'm investing, I look for a stock that's a good year or two-year play. The emphasis in the market on quarter-to-quarter results contributes to the high beta in this sector. I think the people that win tend to be people who are taking a longer-term approach."

It doesn't take a lot of capital to get a software company started. All it takes is a good idea and programming talent. The concept and the skills are easy to identify. There's not much risk in that. The risk begins just as the investor is invited to participate. Besides a great idea and engineering know-how, a software company also needs marketing acumen and distribution channels. Those skills are harder to judge.

It is not easy for start-up companies to get scarce store shelf space if they choose to distribute through retailers or distributors. These resellers have built up long relations with the Microsofts of the software world, and they are cautious about giving up precious trading territory to new and uncertain partners. It's also difficult for a company without a reputation to secure corporate sales. Fortune 500 companies are hesitant to spend major dollars on a young company that may not be around a year or two from now. There is too much at stake.

Stick with What You Know

People who invest in tech stocks are looking for the next hot concept, the next Microsoft. To me, it is Microsoft. I'd much rather go with Microsoft.

From the Experienced Investor

The Microsoft Effect

Remember the character played by Dustin Hoffman in the movie *The Graduate?* His father's business associate told him to buy plastics. The advice today would be buy Microsoft. You can't lose. Spreadsheets, word processing, and database programming were what drove the software business when personal computing first started. Since then, the names of all the dominant companies have changed, except one. Names of powerhouses like WordPerfect, Borland, and Ashton-Tate slipped off everybody's tongue. Where are they today? Today Microsoft owns 80 per cent of its markets with 70 per cent of its profits coming from its Office Suite. Microsoft has consistently traded at 25 times earning and five times sales. Generally only small start-ups have ratios this high and it demonstrates the confidence investors have in Microsoft's growth even at $150 a share.

Microsoft was itself a start-up in Albuquerque, New Mexico in 1975, when it was licensed to provide an operating system for IBM personal computers. At a time when the public conception of a computer was a lumbering machine taking up a large room or a building, Bill Gates's vision for the company was "a computer on every desk and in every home." In its 22 years, Microsoft has come close to realizing its first dream and is on its way to the second. In 1997, Microsoft made $4.56 billion from its Office productivity products, $3.66 billion from its operating systems, $2.46 billion from its back office products, and $960 million from its Internet offerings. In its 1997 annual report, Microsoft said, "Some of the investments we are making in this new area will pay off — others won't. We still have a lot of learning to do."

Microsoft is a good indicator of where technology is going. It is always looking ahead to the next direction and is not reluctant to invest its money in the next trend. It'll take a chance and its chances tend to score. In 1996, analysts were bemoaning the fact that Microsoft didn't seem to have an Internet strategy. Yet, without a hiccup this year, it has managed to overwhelm the Internet market. Just like other investors in technology, it has had its share of losers. But when it has a win, it's a big one.

Using traditional evaluation techniques, one would never invest in Microsoft. It's always been an expensive stock that was probably underdiscounted for risk, and yet if at any point in the last 10 years if you would have put money in Microsoft, you'd be up.

Douglas van Dorsten,
senior technology analyst, Hambrecht & Quist

Beyond Microsoft

Although Microsoft operating systems bundle more and more utilities — disk compression, memory management, anti-virus programs, and screen savers — there is still a demand for third-party utility programs. Symantec, the desktop utility leader, has acquired smaller utility companies like Norton, Central Point Software, Fifth Generation Systems, Contact Software, and Delrina and built a lucrative niche around Microsoft.

Symantec Corporation, founded in 1982 and first public in 1989, actually cooperates very closely with Microsoft. A lot of Symantec's products are utility tools which complement Microsoft's. "We do not take a head-on position against Microsoft," says Lori Barker, Symantec's manager of investor relations and competitive analysis.

Microsoft is always adding to and refining its main products — Windows 95 and Office 97. Over the years, they have added various utilities into their products and then occasionally backed off. For example, at one time Microsoft had a virus checker built into its operating system. The latest Windows systems no longer include that feature and Norton AntiViris has become Symantec's bread and butter product.

Microsoft didn't back away because of a soft spot for Symantec. Some of the Symantec utilities are specialized and not everyone appreciates their precious computer memory cluttered with specialized utilities they will never use. One of the problems Microsoft has with Office 97 is that some users feel it is becoming too large. Symantec considers itself to be in a good position to profit from that sentiment. "People are saying only give us the functionality we need," Lori Barker says. "Don't give us an entire drawer full of silverware. I only want a spoon today. I only want a fork today." The software companies that are able to sit at the Microsoft table make spoons or forks, or they make the ladles and salad tongs that aren't part of the Microsoft silverware collection — yet.

Symantec, for instance, has a very successful product for sales force automation called ACT. When Microsoft released Office 97, it completely revamped its personal information manager, Schedule + until it looked very similar to ACT. Microsoft's new product, Outlook, is a great improvement over Schedule +, but not everybody needs or wants such a powerful PIM taking up a lot of disk space on their hard drive.

To look at the rapidly growing areas of software, step away from the Microsoft Windows desktop applications market and into enterprise-wide computing. You find rapid growth areas through client/server computing which offers the ease of use of the personal computer at the client end, and the sophisticated centralized data administration of a mainframe at the server end. Microsoft contends in this arena with Windows NT and is challenging the troubled Novell Inc. networking software. The demand for corporate database software products offered by Oracle Systems, Sybase, and Informix is growing, and other Microsoft competitors, like PeopleSoft and the German company SAP are packaging their enterprise software into suites for large organizations to include human resources management, corporate accounting, and financial packages.

Because of their complexity, these suites require more training, consulting, and support than the desktop applications. Publicly traded consulting companies like SHL Systemhouse, CGI, EDS, and Andersen Consulting could garner a lot of business from the demand.

Measuring the Worth

Not surprisingly, most large software firms are profitable while most smaller ones are not. Beyond the magnitude of development costs, the other variable costs are relatively low. But once a software firm reaches critical mass, which in this segment means revenues around $30 million, profits rise significantly. Companies which have transcended that critical mass are pretty safe bets. Even when they experience a downtick when they don't meet analysts' quarterly expectations, it doesn't mean the company has changed its fundamentals.

"Balance sheet analysis is probably irrelevant for most software companies, except for cash and accounts receivable," Alex Batula, software analyst for Midland Walwyn Capital Inc., says. "The accounting world doesn't know how to put intellectual assets into a proper accounting perspective."

A software company is a simple business model to understand. Software developers can write a given number of lines of code a day and therefore it is not hard to figure out the cost of development of a software product. So when there are no competitors, the profit margin on the product can be set extremely high. The shares of a typical software company will sell for between three and four times its revenues. When analysing a software company, analysts project its potential price to be 20 to 25 times its forward earnings.

While any software company has to support its established customer base or lose it, it also needs a strategy for the future. While protecting its own customer base, it has to look up to see what opportunities the big guys, like Microsoft, are leaving. At the same time, smaller companies with no installed or established customer base, and no channels, usually have nothing to lose, and can shoot for the moon.

You see the big players survive while revenue growth of the older small companies begins to fall, and all of a sudden the up and coming upstarts hit the market and settle into a niche left open for them. Then the cycle begins again.

Your bread and butter tomorrow, or two years from now, is not going be what you are selling today.

Alex Batula, high-tech analyst, Midland Walwyn Capital Inc.

A Venture Capitalist's View

The successful software companies have very attractive attributes. They can grow to a large size with a relatively small amount of capital. If they do succeed, software companies have good liquidity, which is critical. Apart from being able to deploy capital, you can actually get it out. The gross profit margins in software are still among the highest for any industry in history. These enormous margins let them use internally generated funds to build the companies. Software companies can reinvent themselves and, unlike other industrial organizations or hardware companies, if the strategy is wrong it can be adjusted quickly and they can thrive and prosper.

Loudon Owen, venture capitalist, McLean Watson Capital Inc.

Loudon Owen, together with his partner John Eckert, runs McLean Watson Capital Inc., a venture capital firm that invests successfully in growth-oriented enterprises. His most significant home run to date is SOFTIMAGE, in which he, his partners, and a small group of investors invested $350,000 as the first and only external investors prior to its initial public offering. SOFTIMAGE, which produces high-end software for production of digital media content for the entertainment industries, grew on the strength of this modest investment. It prospered on NASDAQ, and was ultimately sold to Microsoft for $200 million. Each $5,000 investment in 1988 would be worth $3 million today. McLean Watson invests exclusively in software because it is an industry in which you can obtain what economists call "uneconomic returns." In other words, you can make a bundle.

McLean Watson managing partner Loudon Owen says his underlying philosophy in choosing winners is not different to what an individual investor should do when assessing a company in this sector. He warns that investing in technology is labour intensive because of the need to keep up with the dizzying pace of growth. The best companies are expanding rapidly and spinning off new companies constantly.

This is what Loudon Owen looks for when he is assessing a software company:

1. **The market is the paramount consideration.** Is there a defined, growing, international market that exists today? While potential is important, there has to be a tangible sense that a need for a product exists already. It can't be a solution in search of a problem. A limited regional market, Owen says, is definitely not a recipe for growth.

2. **The core technology.** Does the company own a process that is proprietary and protected from replication? Often software companies use other people's tools to build something to fill an immediate need but without the long-term capability to extend the product's usefulness.

3. **A profit-making orientation**. There has to be a successful marriage between the commercial potential and technological supremacy.

4. **Fit**. The company has to fit with your investment objectives. If you expect returns within three to four years and the company realistically has a 10-year time horizon, it's not for you. Always double the amount of time the company tells you it's going to take for you to get a return. You want the company managers to be optimists, but as the investor, take a jaundiced view. "The horizon we expect is five years," Loudon Owen says. "But we are prepared to wait as long as 10."

The Segments within the Segment

Technology is a global market, and especially for software an export strategy is essential for success. Marleau Lemire Securities Inc., in its annual *Canadian High Tech Industry Review*, divides the software subsector into four categories:

- Consumer, mass market, and branded software like Corel and Softkey.

- Utilities, development tools, and enabling software like Cognos and Hummingbird.

- Vertical market software like Accugraph and Geac Computers.

- Information technology services like CGI and EDS.

1. **Consumer mass market and branded software are characterized by**:
   - short sales cycles
   - channels dominated by distributors and retail outlets
   - brand name visibility

- moderate R&D expenditure
- fast product release schedule
- high-growth, high-margin potential
- intense competition, causing price erosion
- solid management teams

2. **Utilities, development tools, and enabling software are characterized by**:

- sales cycles of three to 24 months
- more technical in nature
- channel is direct sales, distributors, and value-added resellers
- high-growth, high-margin potential
- price not the only factor for buyers
- solid management teams
- high market penetration

3. **Vertical market software is characterized by**:

- combination of software, hardware, and services
- products requiring training provided by the company
- long sales cycles
- recurring significant revenue from services
- direct sales channels
- moderate growth and margin potential
- solid management teams

4. **Information technology services are characterized by**:

- services making up bulk of revenues
- long sales cycles
- people main asset
- track record with customers in specific industries is important

Industry Homily

In the software business, your assets are the people who go up and down the elevator every day.

The Software Subsegments

As hard as it is to compare segments within the technology sector, it is equally difficult to compare the subsegments within software. The software landscape is constantly changing as new companies with new ideas advance and older ones recede. The best way to make a fair comparison is to stack similar types of companies against each other. This is a classification of the various subsegments.

- **Powerhouses** — Microsoft plus computer companies with big software divisions

- **Enterprise Applications** — Serving the client-server

- **Utilities and Tools** — Behind the scenes software

- **Document Management** — The paperless society may happen yet

- **Internet and Intranet Tools** — Cool things for the web

- **EDI** — Electronic data interchange

- **Firewalls** — Computer security

- **Graphics and Multimedia** — Creating content

- **Databases** — Relational databases are neat

- **Management Information Systems** — The integrators

- **Accounting Applications** — Streamlining financials

- **Year 2000** — Saving the world from disaster
- **Help Desk, Sales Force Automation** — Making customer service interactive
- **Scientific and Modeling** — Automating design
- **Interactive Games** — Action play and edutainment
- **Niche Players** — The big companies of the future?

```
45...DEG↑365...RKDE↓85...SCEB↑22.34...ITS↓956
```

NICHE SOFTWARE COMPANIES:
ARE THESE THE BIG COMPANIES OF THE FUTURE?

Company	Ticker Symbol
Electronics for Imaging	EFII
McAfee	MCAF
Intuit	INTU
Wind River Systems	WIND
Lernout & Hauspie	LHSPF
Integrated Systems	INTS
Fonix	FONX
Geoworks	GWRX
Rainbow Technologies	RNBO
Inso	INSO
PSW Technologies	PSWT
Xcellenet	XNET
International Microcomputer Software	IMSI
TSR	TSRI
General Magic	GMGC
Insignia Solutions	INSGY
CITATION Computer Systems	CITA
Dataware Technologies	DWTI

TELECOMMUNCATIONS

Growth with Stability

As the economy grows, the phone services grow with it, or even faster. There are so many areas that are still growing: cellular phones, Internet connections, home-office additions. If you're interested in investing in an emerging market, it's an excellent play.

Gene Walden, author,
The Hot 100 Emerging Growth Stocks in America

With solid, reliable companies showing both consistent track records and good growth prospects, telecommunications is the best of all possible worlds. Telephone technology was by far the best performing sector in 1997, despite a couple of very sharp corrections. The world telecommunications market is estimated to be worth $670 billion a year and the US market is valued at about $200 billion.

In most parts of the world, telecommunications is a regulated industry. The Federal Communications Commission (FCC) in the United States, the Canadian Radio-television and Telecommunications Commission (CRTC) in Canada, and similar agencies in other countries set prices and approve competition. Globally, the telecommunications industry is going through a period of deregulation, allowing more competition and awarding licences for more services. This opening of the industry has been encouraging investment by creating new opportunities and establishing new players.

The Telephone Companies

The telephone companies (telcos) have traditionally made up the safe portfolios of widows and orphans because along with the other utilities they were considered to be the most secure investments, never spectacular performers but giving a sure, steady return every year. With nearly 2.1 million registered shareowners, AT&T is the most widely held stock in the United States. Most of the investment in the Bell Canada Enterprises family of companies comes from normally cautious institutions — pension funds, mutual funds, and insurance companies. Robert Ferchat says when he was president of Northern Telecom, the Bell Canada Enterprises equipment-manufacturing wing — about 75 per cent, or 15 million of the 22 million floating shares — were held by institutions. "They're buying it essentially because it's a good, safe bet for the long term."

When institutions invest, they have very little choice but to stay invested. Once they decide to allocate a proportion of their portfolios to telecommunications, the options to move in and out are pretty narrow. Even with deregulation, there aren't that many large telecommunications alternatives. "One of our shareholders has 3 million shares. They had them for 10 years, for God's sake! And they're not about to sell," says Robert Ferchat. With the big institutions sitting tight, it means very small blocks of trade can move a stock price up or down significantly in the course of a day. In fact, even with its large float, Nortel did move two points in the course of one day on a volume of only 2000 shares.

Still solid and steady, the telephone companies' embracing of new technologies has turned them into an engine for phenomenal growth. With a change in management in 1993 and a renewed focus on research and development, Nortel stock charged from a low of $28 to $150 in a relatively short period of time. There are certainly dips and spikes in its performance, but with the telecommunications equipment market expected to grow by $75 billion by 1999, it is hard to imagine that this outstanding performance won't continue. How the telephone companies react to competition in what was once a comfortable monopoly situation will determine their long-term desirability as an investment.

The investors in technology are willing to take a chance, and for that risk they want a bigger win than they would get with the rest of the market. Telecommunications stocks have always been a pretty safe bet with good returns every year, but suddenly the environment they are operating in is exhilarating and spine tingling. For the investor, it is sometimes ironically hard to rationalize that risk can go along with the certainty.

Deregulation

Deregulation is a double-edged sword for the telephone companies. While it catapults them suddenly into a competitive market place, it also reduces restrictions and allows an expansion of services and products. The years of monopoly have generated a culture of complacency for the established telephone companies, and they have been as bureaucratically top-heavy as the most bloated governments. But deregulation is forcing them to learn how to become nimble and cost efficient very quickly.

In Canada, the next step in deregulation brings competition to the local telephone service arena. But the telcos aren't too worried. Their studies project a mere 1 per cent erosion of the local telephone market. But long-distance deregulation cost them 24 per cent of their business, and in other countries the established telephone companies have lost up to 25 per cent of their market when local services were deregulated. But when you have enjoyed a monopoly for so long, it is hard not to be smug.

Deregulation is also allowing the telephone companies to unbundle many of their services. They can slough off the less profitable parts of their business, such as residential service, or charge more for other unbundled parts such as maintenance and repair. With new technologies, especially digital, there are also many more value-added services the telephone companies can charge for: Call waiting, call display, and call answer all run at close to 100 per cent profit for the telephone once the low-cost software programs that generate them are paid for. The Internet has also been a boon to the telephone industry, which provides much of the wiring and connectivity infrastructure no matter who actually sells the Internet products to the ultimate end-user. But the telephone companies have their own fingers in the Internet pie, with interests in many aspects of this data-based computer-to-computer telecommunication.

The new participants brought into the telecommunication market by deregulation also present the investor with other investment challenges. Many are starting out with limited access to cash and without an existing customer base or an established and recognizable brand name. Their success is predicated on their ability to establish a profitable niche and operate more efficiently than their mammoth telco competitors, a formidable challenge.

> Going to the market with the name BCE Mobility versus Brand-X Mobility, we immediately get an audience. Everyone knows BCE. Even though there are no implicit or explicit guarantees, we tend to fare a little better because we're one of the family.
>
> *Robert Ferchat,*
>
> *chairman and CEO, BCE Mobile Communications Inc.*

Now that the new competitors have been in the market for a number of years, the sector is being marked by rejigging as alliances are built and companies grow and divest. Upstart WorldCom Inc., a distant fourth in the long-distance market, with revenues of about $7 billion, a third of second-place Sprint, bought the immense MCI Communications Corp. for a $30 billion, making it the largest merger in corporate history. The Jackson, Mississippi-based WorldCom, struggling to stay afloat as a tiny long-distance company just a dozen years ago, is now a $30-billion company with a budget three times as big as the entire state of Mississippi's. The combination of WorldCom and MCI, already the second-largest US phone company, however, will still not eclipse AT&T Corp., still in first place.

Starting as a tiny long-distance venture called LDDS Communications Inc. (LDDS stood for Long-Distance Discount Service), the company, which went public in 1989, changed its name to the grander-sounding WorldCom in 1995. An investment of $5000 when WorldCom was trading at about $19 would now be worth about $18,000.

For the first time, a single company is within reach of dominating the Internet. Operating in more than 50 countries — with its subsidiaries, UUNET Technologies, Inc. and CompuServe Network Services — WorldCom is the world's largest provider of Internet services. The combined company controls upward of 60 per cent of all US Internet traffic, giving it an unprecedented amount of clout and potential pricing power over the Internet. For years, the Internet has functioned like a commune, with service providers freely exchanging e-mail messages and Web pages between each other's members at no charge. But WorldCom conceivably could step up a drive to charge small Internet-access providers for the right to link to its network.

Telephone Versus Cable

The hot new technologies currently exciting investors involve the distribution of information from one location to another. These technologies, whether in the form of interactive TV, cable PC, or high-definition television, will use telephone, coaxial cable, satellite, and wireless channels. These telecommunications links have become the railroads and tankers of the information age.

The main competition to serve as the delivery system for information appears to be between the telephone companies and the cable companies. Both are massive industries and their spheres of business are moving closer together. Local telephone service in North America brings in $88 billion a year, with revenues growing at 3 to 5 per cent annually. Cable brings in $20 billion, but its growth rate is estimated at 25 to 30 per cent. While the telephone companies have longer experience in two-way communications, coaxial cable is currently the more effective delivery system for interactive services. The telephone companies have a better reputation for customer service, quality, and reliability, and despite the penetration of cable, the larger customer base. Everybody has a telephone. Neither the cable industry nor the telephone industry has distinguished itself as capable of providing content.

However, both coaxial cable and twisted copper telephone wiring will be supplanted eventually by fibre optics. Fibre optics is the transmission of messages or information by light pulses along hair-thin glass fibres. Smaller and lighter than conventional cables of copper wires or coaxial tubes, optical fibres can carry much more information, allowing the transmission of large amounts of data between computers, data-intensive television pictures, and many simultaneous telephone conversations. Optical fibres are immune to electromagnetic interference from lightning or nearby electric motors and to crosstalk from adjoining wires.

"A lot of newcomers coming into the business aren't saddled with the expenses of a legacy installed 40 years ago with central office switches that may be up to 20 years old," says Robert McWhirter, vice-president and portfolio manager for Royal Bank Investment Management. "With what is the equivalent of a brand new sheet of paper, they can install the best equipment at the lowest cost to operate."

As the companies align and realign to develop empires of efficiency, the big story for investors is consolidation and convergence. Building the information superhighway is not cheap, and even the biggest companies struggle with expenditures. Both the telephone and cable companies are eyeing each other's territory with open desire. Mergers and acquisitions are continuing at a fast pace to the benefit of shareholders. Being able to cluster telephone and cable services into one heightens efficiencies in purchasing, marketing, and advertising and enhances the opportunities for new services that fall between both industries.

The Northern Telecom Scenario

Well over 50 per cent of Northern Telecom's products didn't exist five years ago. That's a phenomenal rate of change. They are converting more and more to software, or variations on software. Fifteen years ago, I'd say the bulk of its business was hardware. Now it's the other way around. They're essentially a software firm developing network solutions.

John Drolet, analyst, Yorkton Securities Inc.

Travelling Down
the Information Highway

Already bandwidth has become a familiar term in the modern
world. Measured in bits per second, bandwidth is the measurement of how much data can travel over a circuit in a given period of time. The greater the bandwidth, the greater the amount of
data the circuit can handle, and the faster you can transmit information. With the ever-increasing volume of information being
shipped, bandwidth is becoming a more precious and limited
resource. Bandwidth at the end of the twentieth century might
be what oil was to the 1970s. And speculating in bandwidth
futures could match the energy transaction of the oil crisis.

One solution to bandwidth scarcity is the shift to fibre
optics. The hairlike fibre optic wire can increase the rate of bit
delivery from kilobits per second to gigabits per second, from a
thousand to a million.

Corning Glass Works, famous for its ceramic cookware, is
the world's leading manufacturer of optical fibre, with 35 per
cent of the worldwide market and 50 per cent of the American
market. A driving force behind the communications revolution
since its invention in 1983, fibre optics has propelled the success
of this $4.2 billion company. Fibre optics and the specialty mate-
rials division of Corning account for almost 70 per cent of its
sales and more than 85 per cent of its profits. With earnings
growing at 35 per cent a year since 1994, analysts estimate the
demand for fibre will continue to grow about 25 per cent a year
for the next three years as the phone companies and the cable
operators lay miles and miles of fibre optic cable.

It is regulation that will continue to determine the winners
and the losers. The regulators have both eased and tightened regulations to fine-tune the degree of competition and the level of
service. But even as the regulatory environment relaxes, the gov-

ernment will continue to influence the performance of the contenders. Telecommunications has become essential to our way of life, and as the demand increases, even the most laissez-faire governments will be forced to ensure the fairness of the supply. Understanding of how to manipulate regulatory law might matter even more than knowledge of technology.

Movies on demand, on-line education, interactive banking, and gambling were supposed to push the demand for telecommunications services forward. While the technology is available, so far the demand for these services has not been there at the prices offered.

45...DEG↑365...RKDE↓85...SCEB↑22.34...ITS↓956

TELECOMMUNICATIONS COMPANIES

Company	Ticker Symbol
AT&T	T
SBC Communications	SBC
MCI	MCIC
WorldCom	WCOM
Sprint	FON
Tele-Communications	TCOMA
Teleport Communications	TCGI
Qwest Communications	QWST
Excel	ECI
LCI International	LCI
Andrew Corp	ANDW
McLeod	MCLD
Brooks Fiber Properties	BFPT
Tel-Save Holdings	TALK
Cable Design Technologies	CDT
Intermedia	ICIX
ICG Communications	ICGX
Pacific Gateway Exchange	PGEX

```
45...DEG↑365...RKDE↓85...SCEB↑22.34...ITS↓956
```

IDT	IDTC
Adelphia	ADLAC
American Communications Services	ACNS
Optical Cable	OCCF
SmarTalk Teleservices	SMTK
U.S. Long Distance	USLD
GST Telecommunications	GST
Tollgrade	TLGD
CellularVision USA	CVUS
NACT Telecommunications	NACT
SpecTran	SPTR
CAI Wireless	CAWS

WIRELESS WORLD

Wireless will be the primary growth instrument of telecommunications in the future.

Robert Ferchat, chairman and CEO,
BCE Mobile Communications Inc.

The wireless world of mobile computing and telecommunications includes cellular phones, paging devices, personal communication systems (PCS), mobile radio dispatch used by taxis and the trucking industry, wireless data networks, and satellites. Wireless networks can do such mundane but essential tasks as tracking the levels in propane tanks, the movement of gates at railroad crossings, or monitoring soft drink vending machines.

At the end of 1995, there were 125 million wireless subscribers worldwide. If trends continue, by 2010 there will be about 1.45 billion wireless subscribers, outnumbering wireline subscribers by half a billion. In Canada, where the cellular industry only began in 1985, there are already a total of over 6 million wireless users, including 3.6 million cellular subscribers, 1 million two-way radio dispatch users, and 1 million paging users.

Over $3 billion has been invested in wireless communications infrastructure over the past 10 years.

For investors, the challenge is assessing just how big the market can grow. The number of cellular users is increasing by over 30 per cent a year, so it is estimated, along with the other emerging wireless segments, approximately 40 per cent of the Canadian population will be wireless subscribers within the next 10 years. "Most of the people who invested in it underestimated the popularity of cellular communications," says Robert Ferchat, chairman and CEO of BCE Mobile. "They thought it would be a niche service and it turned out to be a very broadly based one."

Wireless opens up portable access to the existing wired telephone, and any revenues generated by a wireless phone call have to be shared with the telephone company. It is no wonder the telephone companies are so avidly involved in the wireless industry. In the case of the old wired monopolies, like Bell Canada Enterprises, the regulator dictated how much could be earned. The wireless world is a competitive market place and, as such, there is no rate regulation. In a competitive market place, competition is expected to make sure the prices are reasonable both for the user and the supplier.

Far more relevant is that the regulator ensure that the industry remains viable and competitive. When the long-distance industry began in Canada, the regulatory structure allowed anyone to start a long-distance company. The result was an industry with over a hundred new competitors, virtually all of which lost tons of money. "The average investor should know that wireless has the right regulatory structure," says Robert McFarlane, chief financial officer of Clearnet Communications Inc., one of the new competitors. "The success of firms will be dictated by their marketing execution and prowess and not whether there is a favourable regulatory ruling or not."

The Cellular Companies

Until now, the wireless industry has been synonymous with cellular telephone services, with only two licencees in each jurisdiction. The "A" carrier, the nonwire cellular company, operates in radio frequencies from 824 to 849 Mhz, and the "B" carrier, the wireline cellular carrier, usually the local telephone company, operates on the frequencies 869 to 894 Mhz. It is hard to differentiate between the products, services, and features of the duopoly in Canada, the "A" carrier, AT&T Cantel, and the "B" carrier, Bell Mobile Communications Inc. With increasing commoditization, the only competition is on price, and ultimately this depresses margins, earnings, and stock prices. Nonetheless, the shares of the cellular companies are trading well up.

Volume is what drives success in the wireless world, and the most aggressive, best financed will end up being the winners. The cellular companies want to compile as large a subscriber list as possible since it is easier to keep a subscriber than acquire one. Adding subscribers is like buying an annuity. While there are no immediate profits garnered from them because of the competitive price structure, there is long-term revenue potential.

In Canada, there are all kinds of promotions and discounts to secure these customers. Rates are lower than the cost of business, and free phones are routinely offered to encourage signing on. The US is a slightly more mature market. The level of subsidization by the cellular industry is declining, and the American cellular companies are starting to see material improvements in margins and earnings, and in some cases, even profits.

It costs a lot to build a cellular network, and it takes quite a while to recoup the investment. Stock prices have always been based on a multiple of operating cash flow rather than on nonexistent earnings. Finally, in the past three years, established cellular companies in the US have been in a position where there is positive cash flow, and in the last year or so, some of them have been flirting with net income profitability. Investors are examining current performance as well as potential growth and are finally starting to evaluate the wireless companies on the more traditional price to earnings multiple.

PCS: the New Kid on the Block

In the first round of licensing of cellular providers, each region ended up with two competitors, one generally an offshoot of the existing wired telephone company, and the other often associated with the local cable company. Since the advent of digital cellular and personal communications systems (PCS), the number of competitors in each region has increased. "In the old world, if you wanted to invest in wireless you basically had two public cellular companies that more or less followed the same strategy," says Robert McFarlane, CFO of Clearnet Communications. "One couldn't do any worse than to get 40 per cent of market share and the other 60 per cent. By investing in wireless, you were betting on a sector as opposed to a firm. With four competitors, it will now matter whether you are picking the right horse."

In December 1995, in addition to the existing cellular providers in Canada, Clearnet Communications and Microcell Telecommunications Inc. were each granted a licence for a personal communications system with its enhanced wireless services. While they are assured attractive profit margins on the air-time billings, to get there they will have to invest significant sums of money in building a network and developing an organization. With more competitors looking to secure a customer base at any cost, the companies, and their investors, have to be prepared to incur significant negative cash flow for at least the first three to five years of operation. It will be a long time before the red ink changes to black.

"We don't expect to be cash flow profitable for three to four years, and we would not expect to be net income profitable for another seven to eight years," says Robert McFarlane, chief financial officer for Clearnet Communications Inc. "Our company would typify a very long-term investment horizon."

The model for the new PCS companies are their competitors, the established cellular operators. In the early years, the cellular companies' stock traded on potential, or perceived potential, based on strategic developments. They developed their subscriber base anticipating that the number of subscribers would ultimately indicate how much cash flow the company could generate. The analysts and investors who use this model to evaluate the worth of the companies call the practice "subscriber loading." The negative side of subscriber loading is what the industry calls churn — the number of subscribers who leave.

"An advantage for a new entrant like Clearnet is that we were born in a competitive environment. The orientation of certain other firms has been that of a monopoly. They have a huge transition to make to have the same entrepreneurial approach to the market place we do," says McFarlane.

The new PCS networks are very similar to the cellular networks, with signals bouncing from transmission tower to transmission tower, each costing up to $600,000 to construct. The cells are much smaller and are, in fact, called microcells. With a higher frequency on the broadcast spectrum and a shorter range, they have to be closer together than the 5- or 10-mile distance needed between conventional cellular cells. It takes about five times as many towers to provide the same service as cellular.

The cost of building the transmission network is staggering. Not everybody wants a transmission tower in their backyard. Complaints about health, safety, and aesthetics are hard to challenge. To assuage the complaints and to save costs of construction, the new PCS companies are pursuing interesting alternatives for the towers. Clearnet signed an agreement with the Canadian Library Association to gain access to the rooftops of 3500 community libraries in Canada. In return, they are giving each library a high-speed Internet connection.

The advantage of PCS over traditional cellular is that the signal is digital rather than analogue. It can be encrypted before transmission to allow for more security and privacy. It also allows transmission into the concrete skyscrapers of downtown, where cellular transmission fades away. Moreover, because they operate at a frequency of 1.8 gigahertz, double that of cellular phones, PCS phones are far better suited for the transfer of data and wireless computing.

Right now, PCS is used largely for the digital transmission of voice at a higher capacity per megahertz. Very soon, however, the driving force in the wireless world will be the transmission of data, with wireless access to the Internet, wireless point-of-service processing, and wireless private in-building telephone exchanges.

"Effectively, we have taken an industry invented for voice and made it more sophisticated," Robert Ferchat says. "It took over a hundred years for data to take over from voice as the primary bit movement on wireline. We're going to mature much faster than wireline did. It'll happen in 15 years."

Self-Confidence

Our stock, BCX, is down today. After 13 years of a winning record, what's causing me to lose? Am I being outspent, outmanaged, outmarketed? The popular view of our industry is of a continuing growth industry. If it is, then who is going to be better able than us to grow faster than the rest of that industry? And other than the romanticism of picking the long shot, I think the investor would pick the company that, over the years, won the most and lost the least. Our stock is underpriced but, hell, we're not going to lose.

Robert Ferchat, chairman and CEO,
BCE Mobile Communications Inc.

The Sky's the Limit

Motorola Corp., listed on the New York, Chicago, London, and Tokyo stock exchanges, has a bundle of diverse wireless technologies, so whatever dominates, Motorola should be part of it. The equipment businesses this telecommunication powerhouse owns includes cellular telephone, two-way radio, paging and data communications, personal communications, and space electronics. It owns 34 per cent of Iridium Inc., an international consortium building a $3.37 billion satellite phone system comprising 66 communication satellites. Motorola sales for 1996 reached $28 billion, with earnings of $1.15 billion.

Of Motorola's sales, 58 per cent were outside the United States. Many feel the best opportunities for wireless communications lie in the international market, particularly the developing world and the former Eastern Bloc countries. While access to a telephone seems to be almost a right in the developed world, it has been estimated that half the people in the world have never had the chance to make a phone call. Because of the cost of building a telephone network where none exists, many developing countries are bypassing the traditional wireline phone system and jumping directly to wireless as their communications infrastructure. While growth in these markets is increasing exponentially with global investing, there are always concerns about civil, political, economic, and regulatory risk.

What long-range investors should look for is a seamless communications network that will combine satellite communications with analogue and digital cellular systems. Today, telephone numbers connect individuals with a specific place, usually an office or a home. Future technologies will eventually provide each person with a single integrated phone number for the communicating of voice, data, and images. With new players and technologies emerging, expect even television broadcasts to be delivered by wireless.

The wireless industry is expected to grow by four to five times over the next 10 years. The odds are certainly with the long-term investor that stock value is going up. But, as is true with every technology sector, be prepared for some dips along the way.

45...DEG↑365...RKDE↓85...SCEB↑22.34...ITS↓956

WIRELESS, CELLULAR, AND SATELLITE COMPANIES

Company	Ticker Symbol
AT&T	T
Lucent	LU
Motorola	MOT
Northern Telecom	NT
Airtouch Communications	ATI
AMP	AMP
Nextel	NXTL
Qualcomm	QCOM
Loral Space & Communications	LOR
Andrew Corp.	ANDW
Scientific Atlanta	SFA
Paging Network	PAGE
Omnipoint	OMPT
Winstar	WCII
Mobile Telecommunications	MTEL
DSP Communications	DSPC
EchoStar Communications	DISH
P-Com	PCMS
Antec	ANTC
Powerwave Technologies	PWAV
Aerial Communciations	AERL
Trimble Navigation	TRMB
Coherent	CCSC
Cellnet Data Systems	CNDS
Cylink	CYLK

`45...DEG↑365...RKDE↓85...SCEB↑22.34...ITS↓956`

Teledata	TLDCF
California Microwave	CMIC
Stanford Telecommunications	STII
Itron	ITRI
Spectrian	SPCT
Interdigital	IDC
CD Radio	CDRD
American Mobile Satellite	SKYC
Advanced Radio Telecom	ARTT
Orion Network Systems	ONSI
Geotek	GOTK
Wavephore	WAVO
Metricom	MCOM
Proxim	PROX
CellularVision USA	CVUS
Wireless Telecom	WTT
Celeritek	CLTK
Anaren Microwave	ANEN
STM Wireless	STMI
Microwave Power Devices	MPDI
CAI Wireless	CAWS
California Amplifier	CAMP
Osicom Technologies	FIBR

NETWORKING

The network is the computer.

Sun Microsystems slogan

In the beginning was the mainframe computer, large, powerful devices as big as a house. Then came the small personal computer individually deployed on the desktop. Then came the drive to connect these individual computers into local area networks so people could share information and work together. The networks became wider and wider, building up to the grandaddy of all networks, the Internet.

Networks are made up of routers and hubs. Routers, the segment dominated by Cisco Systems and 3COM Corp., are the devices that allow networks of different breeds to work together controlling message distribution between optional paths in a network selecting the "best route." Hubs, dominated by Bay Networks and Cabletron Systems, are points of convergence with multiple sockets and intelligent electronics to make sure that if one computer breaks down, it doesn't bring down the whole system. That's what makes up the networking industry, the hottest stock market success of the late twentieth century.

The Cisco Story

All the networking leaders have been growing through mergers and acquisitions. Cisco Systems Inc. was founded in 1984 by the husband-and-wife team of Leonard Bosack and Sandy Lerner, academics who worked at Stanford University. Bosack ran the computers for the Stanford computer science department. Lerner ran the computer system at the business school. In those days, the two computer systems were unconnected, unable to communicate with each other or with any of the other computer systems scattered around the Stanford campus.

The Cisco founders devised the means to connect the different networks, thus creating one big Stanford network. Bosack came up with the crucial innovation: a high-speed, relatively inexpensive "router," a device to forward data from one computer site to another, and the software to allow the data to be read by any kind of computer on the network. If Stanford had not refused them permission to produce routers for Xerox and Hewlett-Packard, it is quite possible they would never have started Cisco. But when Stanford stood in their way, they formed Cisco, and their new technology took them on their way.

To start Cisco, Bosack and Lerner mortgaged their house for seed capital and borrowed against their credit cards. Don Valentine of Sequoia Capital, the legendary Silicon Valley venture capitalist who had financed such home runs as Apple and Oracle, gave Cisco its one and only infusion of venture money in 1987. Most venture capitalists look at the people behind the company and how they will manage the business. In the case of Bosack and Lerner, their management skills were nil. But there was a great potential market for the product, and they already had revenues of $200,000 even before they recruited a sales force. If he was going to raise capital for this innovative company, Valentine stipulated that he be allowed to shape the company's management team.

Lerner and Bosack held on to 35 per cent of the stock while Sequoia Capital received close to one-third, a position that would be worth more than $7 billion today. Unlike many of today's technology start-ups, Cisco soon had both a product and revenues. It did nearly $1.5 million worth of business by the fiscal year that ended in July 1987 and even turned an $83,000 profit. Between 1987 and 1989, Cisco's revenues went from $1.5 million to $27.7 million, with profits of $4.2 million in 1989. The next quarter it made another $2.5 million.

Cisco stock was first issued on February 16, 1990 at a price of $18. In its scant six years as a publicly traded issue, Cisco's stock has split five times, so adjusting for splits, the actual cost of the first issue equals 56 cents, and in 1997, it was trading at $85. Since becoming a public company, Cisco's annual revenues have increased from $69 million to $6.44 billion, nearly one hundredfold in seven years. As measured by market capitalization, Cisco is the third largest company on NASDAQ and among the top 40 in the world.

Cisco's router technology started to become outdated in the early 1990s. Routers were still a hot ticket, but some small companies were already starting to manufacture switches, devices that could automatically divert data along certain connecting paths, somewhat like the principle of transferring railroad cars from one track to another. Cisco, now run by professional managers, saw the new trend coming and countered by acquiring switching pioneer Cresendo Communications, showing that not only was it not wedded to its own technology, but it wasn't even wedded to the idea that it had to invent new technology in-house.

In the end, it turned out that switches didn't replace routers so much as complement them, and today Cisco dominates both markets. With 75 per cent of the routing market, 40 per cent of the switching market, and 80 per cent of all the traffic on the

Internet flowing through its products, Cisco has gross margins of 67 per cent.

The phenomenal success allows Cisco to attract the best engineers, and also gives them the leverage to buy companies that are themselves poised to make their mark in the networking business. In its short existence, Cisco has acquired: Newport Systems; Kalpana; LightStream Corp.; Combinet Inc.; Internet Junction Inc.; Grand Junction Inc.; Network Translation Inc.; TGV Software Inc.; StrataCom Inc.; Telebit Corp.; Nashoba Networks Inc.; Granite Systems Inc.; Netsys Technologies; Telesend; Skystone Systems Corp.; Global Internet Software Group; Ardent Communications Corp.; and Dagaz (Integrated Network Corporation) — all leaders in their networking niche. These names might not be familiar to the average investor, but Cisco picked out the best company in its niche. If investors had picked out the ones that were public, they would be proud and affluent owners of Cisco stock. It has made millionaires of hundreds of Cisco employees, all of whom have stock options, and many of whom expect never to work again after they leave the company. Mutual fund managers have made tremendous sums for their clients with Cisco. The giant Fidelity Investments mutual fund company currently owns about 28 million shares of the stock, more than 10 per cent of the company.

Even in a market fuelled by the success of technology stocks, few have risen as powerfully as Cisco. It is also one of those rare stocks that has caught fire and continued to burn, a rocket of the sort that comes along only once in an investor's lifetime, if that. Just on the fundamentals, there is a lot to like about Cisco. It has a solid management team. It is remarkably lean. Its revenue per employee is among the highest in the technology sector, and as the stock has increased in value, its astonishing $23-billion market capitalization places it behind only Intel and Microsoft on NASDAQ.

We think we can be in this industry what Microsoft has been in the software industry.

John Chambers, CEO, Cisco Corporation

3Com Tries Harder

At $5.5 billion, 3Com Corporation, which stands for Computer Communication Compatibility, is the second big player in the networking business. Like Cisco, it has grown through acquisition, closing 14 deals since it was founded in 1979. Since its amalgamation with Bridge Communications, 3Com acquired BICC Data Networks for $25 million in 1992; Star-Tek for $56 million and Synernetics for $104 million in 1993; Centrum Communications and Nicecom for $95 million in 1994; AccessWorks, Sonix Communications for $70 million, Primary Access for $170 million, and Chipcom for $775 million in 1995, and changed its slogan to "The Global Data Networking Company"; Axon for $65 million, OnStream Networks for $245 million, and U.S. Robotics (the world's leading manufacturer of modems) for $7.3 billion in 1997.

3Com traded on NASDAQ under the symbol COMS for the first time on March 24, 1984 with an initial price of $1.50, adjusted for two stock splits. But 3Com has also been incredibly volatile, its price swinging between $24 and $81 over the past year, reflecting concerns that its adapter card market connecting networks was being outstripped by newer technologies. While more than 50 per cent of 3Com's revenue used to come from the adapter market, it had adapted like Cisco, and over the past few years, less than 40 per cent of its overall revenue comes from the sale of adapters and more and more from systems products.

Manufacturers like Microsoft and Pointcast are writing very resource-intensive applications. As these applications and data are centrally stored in networking environments, the bandwidth required to access them needs to be increased. There is such a demand for higher performance through higher speed devices, it only follows that companies like 3Com are going to be successful and people are going to want to invest and ride on that success.

Patrick Guay, general manager, 3Com Canada

This subsector continues to flourish as the companies attempt to offer networking services and products — such as adapters, routing, switching, Asynchronous Transfer Mode technology, remote access, and network management — all from one source. Both Cisco and 3Com investors have enjoyed joyous rides with one company pushing the other to new acquisitions, new technologies, and greater heights.

Networking stocks have been kind to a lot of people. The question, as we head into the next century, is whether these are buy-and-hold opportunities to pass on to the next generation, or if the networking bubble is ready to burst. But when companies are doing well, they tend to be able to sustain momentum. "Companies surprising on the upside are probably less likely to blow up and more likely to continue surprising on the upside for an indefinite period," says Paul Wick, manager of the Seligman Communications and Information Fund.

45...DEG↑365...RKDE↓85...SCEB↑22.34...ITS↓956

NETWORKING COMPANIES

Company	Ticker Symbol
AT&T	T
Cisco Systems	CSCO
Lucent	LU
Motorola	MOT
Northern Telecom	NT
3Com	COMS
Tellabs	TLAB
Newbridge Networks	NN
Bay Networks	BAY
Ciena	CIEN
Ascend	ASND
ADC Telecommunications	ADCT
DSC Communications	DIGI
Advanced Fibre	AFCI
Andrew Corp	ANDW
PairGain	PAIR
ADTRAN	ADTN
Tekelec	TKLC
Premisys	PRMS
Xylan	XYLN
Yurie Systems	YURI
Teledata	TLDCF
Network Equipment Technologies	NWK
Ortel	ORTL
Digi International	DGII
Digital Link	DLNK
Larscom	LARS
Harmonic Lightwaves	HLIT
General Datacomm	GDC
NACT Telecommunications	NACT
Teltrend	TLTN
Retix	RETX
Verilink	VRLK

```
45...DEG↑365...RKDE↓85...SCEB↑22.34...ITS↓956
```

Computer Network Technology	CMNT
ACT Networks	ANET
Farallon Communications	FRLN
Summa Four	SUMA
FastComm	FSCX
Osicom Technologies	FIBR
Netrix	NTRX

THE INTERNET

The History of the Internet

The Internet, conceived in the 1960s, came to full term in the mid-1990s when it was reported that there were more than 20 million people around the world hooked into it. The idea started as a fail-safe for the United States Department of Defense to protect its computer network from massive bombing. Each part of the network stood alone but could communicate with any other part through a standard communication protocol. This Internet protocol has become the accepted standard for linking computers and networks of all kinds, and it has evolved into a global electronic network for ideas and information.

Though this relentless interconnection of computers had been proceeding over the years, it wasn't until the mid-1990s that the investment community stood up and took notice. When it did, the Internet became everybody's investment darling. As with any new technology, it is the tools, or the plumbing, that get the first attention. In the gold rush, the first people to turn a profit were the ones who sold the picks and axes. The Internet picks and axes — the servers and connectivity devices — are supplied by the industry leaders, Cisco Systems, Hewlett-Packard, Digital, and Sun Microsystems — and their shares that have been skyrocketing during the Internet boom.

The Three Phases of the Internet

You can play the infrastructure and consulting guys — the folks who make the boxes that allow you to connect to the Internet and the consultants — and system integrators that help companies set up on the Internet. The next phase is in the foundation hardware — PC servers such as Compaq, Digital, and Hewlett-Packard, and software like Netscape and Microsoft. The final phase, coming up, are the companies doing application and content development. It might not be the Internet itself, but it is going to be Internet-standard-based information technology, that is going to be the wave that carries the industry with it.

Chip Morris, manager,
T. Rowe Price Science and Technology Fund

It is not only the hardware heavyweights who behold the universe as Internet. Java, Sun Microsystems' new Internet programming language, and the cool applications you can create with it, has created a buzz. But the real Java buzz is the opportunity it gives others to challenge the Microsoft operating systems. Microsoft NT has been successfully invading the territory of the networkers and worrying them to no end. Java is the weapon they hope to use to regain some of their lost ground, since Java as an open system is "operating-system agnostic." Java is the first universal software designed for Internet and corporate intranet developers to write applications that can run on any computer, regardless of the processor or operating system.

Internet Mania

The rush started for Internet stocks in August 1995 with the initial listing of 5 million shares of Netscape Communications at $28 a share. Netscape's product, the Netscape Navigator Web browser, is the tool that users need to explore the content of the Internet's World Wide Web. Netscape was a company with little revenue and no earnings, but by the end of its first trading day, it had reached a market value of $2 billion, approximately $100 a share. Magnifying the pattern of most IPOs, the stock soon went into a tailspin but then shot upward again. At first, there had been a sizeable short position in Netscape. The short sellers were convinced that the inflated interest in a company with little revenue and less earnings was ridiculous. Anticipating a decline in the price, these investors borrowed shares of the company from their brokers, planning to buy them when the price came back down. When the rally continued, they were forced to fill their short position, or buy to cover the shares owing to the broker, pushing the value of the stock even higher.

While the Internet stocks were hot, they certainly weren't being driven on earnings because there were none. The companies had to reinvest their revenues back into the company to create an infrastructure. So instead of multiples of earnings, or even revenues, the investment community started evaluating these companies by multiple of sales. If one company's share price was identified as achieving three-time sales, it was considered a bargain compared to the one at five-time sales. Analysts would compare only within the segment, but compared to the general market, even compared to the technology sector, Internet stocks were way overvalued. The surge affected all Internet stocks, most notably UUNET Technologies, since taken over by WorldCom, and Spyglass. When the surge subsided in December 1995, these Internet stocks had plunged significantly. Netscape proved to be one of the more buoyant of the Internet stocks. It had used its substantial capital to secure a substantial share of the browser market by giving away free copies, primarily to promote the brand, following the example of the cellular providers. Netscape wants to be in a position to promote ubiquity. Once the Netscape browser and the Netscape tool set is widely established, when upgrades or other products come out, there will be a certain level of brand awareness and brand commitment. Revenues will come from the sale of feature-rich, high-priced server software into corporate environments.

The Internet segment remains one of promise and potential but with few measurable successes. Even the on-line services market, including America Online and the Microsoft Network, represents barely $1 billion. They are all counting on on-line commerce and shopping to drive the Internet, but so far, the Internet has been driven by electronic mail and information retrieval, applications that are harder to charge for. While there are between 20 and 30 million people with access to the Internet, only about 2 million use it regularly. One research firm monitoring the on-line services found 40 per cent of subscribers drop off every year and generally don't return. California represents a third of all Internet traffic and Silicon Valley alone accounts for 25 per cent, so with one earthquake the Internet market could drop 30 per cent.

The cable companies provide an interesting reference for evaluating Internet service providers. Because cable is a mature market, the growth in the number of subscribers there is substantially lower than among Internet users. However, the churn rate is higher in the Internet market since customers have not developed any brand loyalties, and nothing stops them from moving on for a better price or other incentive. As the hype about the Internet has subsided, so have subscriber growth rates. One result has been a consolidation of Internet service providers with Internet services becoming one more offering from the large telecommunications companies such as Bell Canada's Sympatico and Sprint's Internet Passport.

Fooling Around

The first applications for new technologies are always in fun and games. The initial uses of computer chips were in the development of video games, and new chips, like Intel's Pentium MMX, enhance the visuals for computer games. The technology trail leads from fun and games to business to consumers, as you will see in the next chapter. So you have to be sure you are at the right time in the cycle to cash in.

It's no accident that the most successful applications on the Internet are entertainment-style sites. By far the most widely-used and profitable sites are pornography sites, none of which are publicly traded. The next most popular, but not yet profitable, are investment sites. One recent breakthrough in Internet technology is live video. Most mainstream Web sites haven't chosen to offer live video because the moving images are decidedly fuzzy and choppy. For the Internet fun seeker, the stakes are so low they aren't afraid to try the latest. It doesn't matter if an application crashes, it is not as if there is a multimillion-dollar contract at stake.

Finding a Business Model

> So far, nobody is making money off of the Web. In fact, we are in a transition stage and people are scared as hell they'll never be able to learn how to make money.
>
> *Rick Serafini, manager, Trimark Discovery Fund*

The Internet companies see three possible ways for revenues: subscription fees, pay-for-use, or selling advertising. Yahoo, the popular Internet directory service, is staking its future on advertising. It charges advertisers $20,000 a month to advertise on their pages, which it says get between 250,000 to 300,000 hits a day. Yahoo says it already has more than 60 advertisers with revenue opportunities in the tens of millions of dollars. A major selling point is that the ads can be tailored to consumers in novel ways: click on a computer-related subject, and up pops a Microsoft pitch. But a major selling block is that measuring the number of hits has not been accepted by the advertising community as a measure of the buyer's behaviour. Even Microsoft Corporation's annual report for 1997 says, "Just like everyone else on the Web, we don't know what the mix of revenue will be — subscription, advertising, or promotions."

Sceptical advertising people advise their clients to advertise on the Web as loudly as possible but spend as little as possible. Those who are not keen on the Internet claim it is a technology not a medium, in the same way that the printing press is a technology. It's only when the technology is used to create material people want that it will become a medium advertisers are interested in. In the same way, when advertisers consider the content offered by a television station or a magazine before they sign up, they are examining whether the content on the Internet will be engaging.

"This doesn't mean that advertising won't work on the Internet, although it certainly does not seem to be performing to the potential that has been predicted for it," says David Harrison, president of Harrison, Young, Pesonen & Newell, the largest independent media-buying company in Canada. "If you look at who the 10 largest Internet advertisers are, they are basically search engines and software companies. I don't think you're going to find Procter and Gamble advertising Tide, though P&G might have a Web site about how to wash clothes. People who believe they will make a billion or a trillion dollars from the Internet are going to be disappointed."

Charging people for access through subscription or pay-for-use probably isn't the answer either. Despite Pay-TV, information is a commodity which basically has always been presented as being free to the consumer, or at a minimal cost. Newspapers and magazines certainly don't support themselves by charging their readers. Savvy media types talk about buying their readers' time, not selling them a newspaper. This approach hasn't downloaded to the Internet yet.

PointCast Inc. is often cited as a successful Internet model. Still a privately held company, PointCast has received more than $48 million in funding from three technology venture capital firms as well as from nine strategic media and technology partners. PointCast is a news network you can download free from the Internet with information that appears instantly on your computer screen. PointCast broadcasts national and international news, stock information, weather, and sports. It is the first incarnation of what is called in the Internet business Push Technology. You don't have to surf the net for information; it comes to you. The PointCast Network is advertiser supported, with no subscriptions or purchases required by the user. From an investor's perspective, the PointCast model is risky. It is only as good as the content its hard copy partners — CNN, CNNfn, *Time*,

People, and *Money* magazines, Reuters, *LA Times, New York Times, Boston Globe, San Jose Mercury News,* and *The Globe and Mail* — can offer. In order to be accessible for all, PointCast has to encourage open standards, making the concept very easy for others to replicate. Microsoft or Netscape could compete at any time. The giant Microsoft Network is poised to do just that.

While networking has been good to investors, the Internet has not been as kind. Due to the low barriers to entry, the possibility of competition always looms. The lack of a feasible business plan for many Web-related firms has also stunted the rewards. The latest technology catchphrase is Intranet, referring to the application of Internet technologies behind the security firewall within an organization. Even in this more focused niche, except for the companies offering infrastructure, profitability has been elusive.

Fierce competition has been pushing prices down, pressuring the Internet service providers (ISPs) until their viability as stand-alone businesses is in question. Those investors making more on ISPs are short-sellers. Subscriber growth has been slowing and is well below the early inflated projections. The telephone companies entering the arena are offering cut-rate Internet access as a way of generating added revenue for their existing product lines. Though this adds value for their customers, even the telecommunications giants have not yet found a way for the Internet to add to their bottom line. But with convergence and consolidation, the telephone companies are controlling access to the Internet.

The lustre is off Internet stocks, though some, like Netscape, have maintained their value. The newer offerings offer flimsier opportunities, and if the Internet goes the way of the CB radio, as the pessimists suggest it will, so do the investors' funds. Caution is advised.

Not everybody is that pessimistic. T. Rowe Price manager
Chip Morris still likes the Internet. "Our investment play on the
Internet is not on the Internet per se. It's about the standards that
enable the network. Internet-based standards are going to be the
most significant driver of electronic computing over the next
three to five years. There is so much brainpower focused on how
to leverage the Internet and how to make money off it, someone
is going to find the solution and make a lot of money."

```
45...DEG↑365...RKDE↓85...SCEB↑22.34...ITS↓956
```

INTERNET SERVICE PROVIDERS

Company	Ticker Symbol
Microsoft	MSFT
AT&T	T
WorldCom	WCOM
MCI	MCIC
Sprint	FON
America Online	AOL
At Home	ATHM
Compuserve	CSRV
IDT	IDT
American Communications Services	ACNS
PSINet	PSIX
Mindspring Enterprises	MSPG
Netcom	NETC
Earthlink Network	EKNK

`45...DEG↑365...RKDE↓85...SCEB↑22.34...ITS↓956`

INTERNET TOOLS

Company	Ticker Symbol
Microsoft	MSFT
Adobe Systems	ADBE
Novell	NOVL
Netscape	NSCP
Sterling Software	SSW
Lycos	LCOS
Open Market	OMKT
Edify	EDFY
Object Design	ODIS
Elcom International	ELCO
Open Text	OPTEXF
Cybercash	CYCH
Versant Object Technology	VSNT
NetManage	NETM
BroadVision	BVSN
Quarterdeck	QDEK
Spyglass	SPYG
Interleaf	LEAF
FTP Software	FTPS
Visigenic Software	VSGN
Verity	VRTY
ForeFront	FFGI
Connect	CNKT
OneWave	OWAV

FUN AND GAMES

The convergence of the personal computer, the television set, and the telephone will at some point in the not-so-distant future provide the consumer with first-run movies and new music releases, edutainment, interactive games, and on and on, without the potato ever leaving the couch.

Quincy Jones, composer, record, film, and TV producer, arranger-conductor, record company executive, and multimedia entrepreneur

Entertainment and Media

Hollywood meets Silicon Valley. The media moguls want to own the entire entertainment food chain from content creation to distribution. By controlling both production and distribution, they will be able to deliver entertainment across many media, including cinema, television, print, video games, and the so-called new media — the Internet and CD-ROMs. Players from the purer technology side are dipping their fingers into this financial honey pot. The omnipresent Microsoft, along with NBC, has created MSNBC, and is investing heavily in interactive TV and cable television.

With its reliance on new technologies, movies are becoming increasingly more expensive to make, averaging more the $50 million each. Yet every year, the public spends more and more to go to the movies and even more on videotape rentals. As the studios find themselves swinging between boom and bust, they are becoming more dependent on blockbuster hits, most of which feature special effects as a big part of the draw. Many of the traditional production techniques, including cel animation, lighting, image processing, compositing, and editing, are produced digitally on supercomputers like Silicon Graphics Inc. workstations using advanced 3-D graphics capabilities.

The cutting edge of software and hardware technology, once the domain of science and engineering, is now geared for cinematic special effects and commercials. And the $4-billion editing market has shifted to digital-based systems dominated by Avid Technology Inc. Avid's editing systems are software-based, although its commanding share of this growing market is threatened by Sony and Panasonic as they introduce digital videotape.

Hollywood geniuses like Steven Spielberg and George Lucas are now known as much for their technical expertise as their storytelling abilities. The companies they founded — Steven Spielberg, Jeffery Katzenberg, and David Geffen's DreamWorks SKG and George Lucas's Industrial Light and Magic — are becoming digital-effect houses. Paul Allen and Bill Gates, the co-founders of Microsoft, have made a sizeable investment in DreamWorks SGK.

With everybody into everybody else's business, Hollywood thinks it can design games and Silicon Valley thinks it can produce movies. Silicon Valley is always presenting ideas to Hollywood about how to make better movies using digital technology.

But both communities talk about a language barrier. When they were and technology enthusiast Mike Backes as the display graphics supervisor, in effect a liaison between the movie world and the computer world. He remembers a meeting between Silicon Graphics, Inc. and members of the production team, including director Steven Spielberg, where he says he felt like "the only bilingual person in the room" who could converse about both technology and the movie.

Globalization is also an imperative. Rupert Murdoch's News Corp. is the business model most media competitors would like to follow. His empire, constantly changing, includes in the US: a movie studio, Twentieth Century Fox; a television network, Fox TV; a cable network; *TV Guide*; the HarperCollins book publishing company; and the *New York Post*. In Europe, it consists of the Sky pay-TV satellite operation; *The Sunday Times*; *The Times*; *The Sun*; and *News of the World*. In Asia, he owns the direct broadcast operator Star TV, which reaches 350 million TV households with English and local-language programming for sports, music, movies, and general entertainment shows.

Interactive television is perceived as the wave of the future. Viewers will be able to actively play along with the game shows they are watching. Sporting events will offer explanations of the rules and custom-designed statistics, as well as the opportunity to purchase team merchandise at the touch of a button. Video on demand will allow users to scroll through menus of movies and television programs, and instant-access video shopping will offer a full range of products and services.

"These companies use some of the new technologies, but they are not primarily in that game." says Doug Kirk, communications and media analyst at Nesbitt Burns Inc. But technology is making the new information businesses harder for investors to follow. "In the industrial sectors, to measure the value of a company to shareholders, you can count the number of units that are shipped. Knowledge-based assets are less tangible and more difficult to assess," he says.

Venture capitalist Loudon Owen, who financed SOFTIMAGE, which produces software for the entertainment industries, says there are huge ongoing opportunities in this growing sector. He draws a clear distinction between what he calls proprietary and non-proprietary content. Following Rupert Murdoch's model, that means maximizing the reusable material produced by the different media in the group — television, movies, newspapers, and books — and distributing it digitally around the world through the other media. Through quick, inexpensive digital transmission, this content, in which the company must hold clear copyright, can be sold again and again across the media spectrum, adding value to the investment. As copyright legislation evolves to establish the ownership of intellectual property, the content providers will offer the engine for value appreciation in an already lucrative industry.

A Case History: Nelvana

Nelvana Limited, the Canadian animation studio which made *Babar*, *The Care Bears*, and *The Velveteen Rabbit*, is one of those entertainment companies that is relying more and more on technology. As an international distributor to the global television market place, it has amassed a library of inventory it can sell again and again. Animation never goes stale and is not bound by language barriers.

Animation lends itself more to the overlap with technology than any other part of the entertainment business. One of the reasons Nelvana went public three years ago was to invest in new technology that would give it the ability to computer paint its own shows. Painting animation cels is very labour intensive and many of the best-known domestic animated programs, like *The Simpsons*, are actually finished abroad in developing countries, where labour is cheap. Nelvana is now able to paint 40 per cent of its shows in-house rather than shipping the work to Asia, where it has less influence over day-to-day quality control. "By repatriating the work, we have made more money ourselves," says Nelvana co-CEO Michael Hirsch. "We make money on work we do and end up with a reusable digital master that is cleaner and neater than the traditional method."

To keep abreast of technological change, Nelvana invested in a Minneapolis-based company called Windlight Studios, specialists in 3-D computer animation. Along with Medialab, a French computer animation company, Nelvana is co-producing *Donkey Kong Country*, based on the Nintendo video game character. "That will be our first computer animation series," Hirsch says. "We've got a look for the show that's equivalent to the video game but that comes alive and is fully animated."

When Michael Hirsch talks to investors, he knows they are just as fascinated by the technology as they are by the movies. The interest in technology is a signal to them that the company is future-oriented. "It means something to our investors," he says. "Every day that goes by, we move into the technology sector more and more."

But Nelvana's main assets are still its cartoons and the appeal of the characters. However, thanks to the use of digital technology, they are able to accumulate ancillary revenues through the enhanced longevity of their library. "We still focus on our main product line, our shows," Michael Hirsch says. "But over the next few years, I would say that there is going to be a significant technology component, and that component is growing."

Video Games

This interactive entertainment business is still dominated by Sega Enterprises and Nintendo, the Double Dragons from Japan, though the third competitor, Sony, has made inroads. The whole sector is estimated to be worth more than $10 billion. Market share is dependent on which company has the hottest games and the most technologically advanced system. In 1996, with worldwide sales of $3.5 billion, Nintendo, with its Nintendo 64 platform, had 52.3 per cent of hardware units sold, Sony Playstation was at 35.4 per cent, and Sega Saturn had fallen to 12.24 per cent. While Sony, for that year, dominated the Japanese market, Nintendo owned the North American market.

In its first year over 2 million game players bought the Nintendo 64 gaming system despite a drought of software titles. In an average week near Christmas, about 10 games are released for each system.

More and more, the media conglomerates, such as Disney and Time/Warner, are starting to make the bulk of the actual games themselves. They are retaining the rights to the video game licences for their products rather than farming them out to the third-party developers. But licencing is also going the other way. Successful video games are emerging as movies or television shows. The *Mario Brothers* television show and the *Street Fighter* and *Mortal Kombat* movies both added to the coffers of the game creators.

Some of the best opportunities in this sector come from investing in the content providers, such as Acclaim or Electronics Arts, rather than the hardware manufacturers. There are 14 companies in the software group, which includes heavyweights like Disney and Microsoft, and smaller companies such as 7th Level and Spectrum Holybyte.

The interactive software business has historically been highly volatile. The instability of the yen to dollar currency exchange adds significantly to the risk of Japanese hardware companies. More than most technology segments, it is cyclic, radically affected by changing technologies, competition, component supply, consumer spending, and seasonality. Christmas, of course, is the busy season. If the hardware manufacturers — notably Sega and Nintendo, and now Sony — come out with a new platform that catches on for that season, then business booms. But just like in the entertainment business, you're only as good as your last hit. Video game players don't feel any loyalty to any particular game creator; they want to play the latest and hottest game, no matter who makes it, although sequels to hits like *Mortal Kombat* or *Street Fighter* score big. Competition for creative talent to devise the next hit is intense and the attraction and retention of these key people is increasingly difficult.

Typically the toughest competition for the software developers comes from the hardware manufacturers. With their greater financial, technical, and distribution resources, they aggressively promote their own product lines, which contend directly with the games their licensees create. Adding to their woes, the software developers must pay royalties, and in some cases manufacturing charges, to these platform maker.

Traditionally, new technologies, as we saw in our discussion of the Internet, make their first appearances in fun and games. It's not surprising since entertainment applications are easier to develop, and if something goes wrong, the consequences are not that disastrous. If the technology fails when you are flying a jet aircraft, it is much more serious than if you are playing a flight simulator game.

The first experience most of the general public ever had with computer technology were early arcade video games like Atari's *Pong*. As the technology evolved, video games moved into the home as set-top boxes hooked up to the television. Then, as computing processing power increased from 8-bit, to 16-bit, to 32-bit, to 64-bit, the graphics and the speed of play improved and so did the rivalry. The technological evolution has proven to be both a curse and blessing to the video game industry. Young gamers didn't expect much out of games; the graphics and the ideas, though primitive, were novel, so they seemed like fun. As the industry matured and the players grew up, it became harder to please them. The demanding game players wanted grit, rough edges, and attitude. The more realism, the better.

This realism may well be the downfall of video games. As games become more advanced, more attention will be spent on the technological aspects rather than the harder to define game play. Games could become so realistic, so highly evolved that there will be no difference between them and everyday life. They won't offer the escape young people are looking for.

With enhanced graphics and CD-ROMs, the personal computer is emerging as a competitive gaming platform but with nowhere near the penetration of dedicated video games. Computer games are more intellectual than video games and less concerned with manual dexterity, missing the essential interest of the core teenage audience. The PC's greatest advantage is its future as computers are tweaked, fine-tuned, and remodelled for graphical quality. The other advantage PCs have over stand-alone video games is on-line gaming. Microsoft, Intel with its MMX mutlimedia chip, and the cable operators are hoping to use computer games as the wedge that will attract young people to interactive television.

More important to success is the entertainment value to the player than the technology. With *Mortal Kombat* and *Donkey Kong Country*, Nintendo, Sega, and Sony and their creative partners have figured out what emotional triggers will attract teenage boys to Nintendo 64, Sega, Saturn and Sony PlayStation. Once they produce a winner, they build on it with sequels. The Japanese video game developer Capcom started with *Street Fighter* and followed it with *Street Fighter II*, *Street Fighter Turbo*, *Street Fighter Hyperfighting*, *Street Fighter Championship*, and a game based on the movie *Street Fighter Versus X-Men*.

There are good signs for the video game segment. With artificial intelligence and virtual reality, the scope of possibilities for new games and investments is extensive. Hardware sales have been brisk, and there are indications that the new games — among them *Street Fighter III* — are strong. With the increased cost of developing successful products, expect industry consolidation.

Multimedia

Multimedia refers to the use of computers to integrate text, audio, graphics, and animation into specific programs. Applications range from video conferencing and enhanced training simulations to next-generation video games, along with production of education and reference CD-ROMs. In order to work with multimedia, a personal computer needs a powerful microprocessor with a lot of memory and storage capabilities, a high-quality monitor and a video accelerator, external speakers or headphones and a sound card, and a CD-ROM drive. It also requires special software to incorporate external devices, such as a microphone or keyboard for audio input and a video cassette recorder or camcorder for video input or output.

With tools for painting, drawing, visualization, simulation design, animation, and video and audio editing, there is plenty of scope for multimedia implementation. The very fast CD-ROM capabilities, graphics and digital video acceleration, and sophisticated sound boards of the hardware provides the platform for this multimedia proliferation.

Now multimedia developers are turning their attention from entertainment to the business market, trying to increase the integration of multimedia in sales, marketing, and business applications. Presentation software has evolved from simple slide shows run from the personal computer to programs that include video clips, sound, and animation. The next step driving business multimedia promises to be video conferencing — transmitting multimedia images from location to location via telecommunications. Intel has aggressively committed to multimedia, adapting its latest chip (the MMX) for maximum multimedia capabilities.

Accelerated product cycles, low barriers to entry, and the race to set standards make multimedia software one of the most intensely competitive areas. As always, Microsoft is a major player in this segment, and other software companies such as Corel, Adobe, Autodesk, and Micrografx are vigorous in their zeal to compete. Some, most specifically IBM, Kurweil Applied Intelligence Inc., and Dragon Systems Inc., are experimenting with the operation of the computers themselves incorporating voice activation. This lets people use their voice instead of their fingers to do a variety of tasks on their computer, including voice-typing letters, reports and e-mail messages, opening and closing computer files, and navigating the desktop. For home or business users who frequently generate large amounts of text, it's an attractive alternative to the keyboard and mouse. Voice recognition, just at the cusp of wide acceptance, is an illustration of the ephemeral nature of the software business. Dragon Systems, 25 per cent owned by Seagate Technology, used to be the leader in voice recognition with a product that sold for $3000. It is now competing with the IBM Voice-Type that retails for $99.

By developing the right business relations and pushing products quickly to market, developers have a chance to be successful. However, because of the advanced nature of the applications, the risk remains high, with some companies destined to become standard setters and establish large markets for their products, and others bound to fall by the wayside.

Consumer Electronics

Vive la Difference

The difference between a computer and a TV is that you sit close to the former and far away from the latter. You'll sit close when you need to type, do homework, or pay the bills. You'll sit far away when you're at a meeting, or your family wants to watch a movie. You won't see the separation that exists today in these two delivery structures.

Bill Gates, CEO, Microsoft Corporation

Sony Corporation, the consumer electronics, computer technology, media, and semiconductor company, has introduced WEB-TV, a set-top box for your television which offers Internet capabilities including e-mail. With the Sony Internet Terminal, you can surf using a simple remote control and a full television screen with flicker-free picture quality and digital stereo sound. There's a connector for use with printers and cable modems as well as a "smart card" slot for shopping, banking, and other interactive transactions in the future.

At the same time, ATI Technologies Inc. has introduced the All-In-Wonder, a single card to act as the ultimate communications hub uniting TVs and VCRs with the PC. You can sit on the couch and watch TV, browse the Web, and flip to a favourite 3-D video game on a large screen TV, all with the click of a mouse. It lets you keep an eye on what's on TV while you're working on the computer. Users can program "hot words" into a search engine, and when those words appear in the TV's closed captioning, the user is alerted to pay attention.

Both of these are examples of cross-media convergence, the integration of various industries including computers, consumer electronics, publishing, television, and telecommunications melding the multimedia content of these various industries. Technology developed by the consumer electronics industry is increasingly crossing over to computers and back again.

For the technology companies, it means cutting costs to meet the competition from the consumer electronic companies. Profit margins for televisions, stereos, and VCRs are significantly lower than the margins for computers and their components. MIT professor Nicholas Negroponte, author of *Being Digital*, argues that PC prices are artificially high, creating a barrier to making the PC a mainstream consumer appliance. He is on what he calls a "cost arrogance crusade," claiming that hardware and software vendors conspire to keep prices inflated, in the $2000 range, when he thinks they should be in the $200 range. For the technology investor, lower prices would mean lower returns per unit sold, but also create new opportunities as the computer industry broadens its product line to a mass market and figures out how to make off-the-shelf consumer technology viable.

Convergence

Synergy between the two industries will help speed technology development, but the key to growth will come from those companies responsive to convergence. We can already read e-mail on the TV, watch movies from a PC, listen to stereo sound from a CD-ROM drive, and access the Internet from a telephone. The lines of distinction between the two industries are blurring. Convergence is an opportunity, in the view of some, for consumer electronics to leapfrog the computer industry and propel us into the next generation of computing. Computer scientist Alan Kay, vice-president of research and development at Walt Disney Imagineering, calls this "intimate computing."

Consumer research conducted by the Consumer Electronics Manufacturers Association shows that consumers are interested in, and willing to buy, converging products. Thirty-one percent of people surveyed expressed a strong interest in buying a combination television and personal computer. Of those interested in purchasing a TV/PC, 59 per cent said they would use the product for word processing, while 50 per cent said they would browse the Internet or play video games. When they were asked where they would purchase a TV/PC, 56 per cent said they would go to an electronic superstore such as Best Buy, Circuit City, or Future Shop, while 18 per cent said they would get it at a computer superstore.

Technology investors should be hoping the converging products will be bought in computer stores because with the major consumer electronic companies like Sony and Mitsubishi closely held in Japan, there is less opportunity to invest in the stock. With a price to cash flow of 7 to 1, Sony, a $43-billion electronics and entertainment giant which is cross-traded on the New York Stock Exchange, is strikingly inexpensive. If it were based in San Diego instead of Tokyo, every manager in America would buy it. There is a wariness about investing in a Japanese company despite the obvious appeal of its well-known brand name.

MIT professor Nicholas Negroponte sees the blending of the computer and consumer electronic industries as an inversion of the information technological innovation process. He believes technological innovation is now driven first by consumer electronics, and then finds its way back to the computer industry. As a powerful example, he cites the Gulf War, where the US Army could not supply global positioning devices to its combat troops, who ended up buying them from stereo stores in the United States.

DVD

Converging products like TV/PCs and digital videodiscs (DVD) are transforming our attitude to technology. There are those investors who think DVD, and not the Internet, will alter the technology and entertainment landscape. DVD are super-CDs, and could replace videotapes, audiotapes, and CD-ROMs over the next few years. Indistinguishable from a CD-ROM, a DVD will hold between seven and 25 times as much data and could help bring television-like graphics and sound to the PC.

The tremendous storage capacity is what makes DVD so powerful. A movie company, for example, could dub a disc with as many as eight different language tracks, or offer 32 sets of subtitles. And while software manufacturers now deliver their product on CD-ROMs, they'll be able to offer much more on DVD-ROMs, which hold at least as much data as 3,450 floppy disks.

While the rival camps on the consumer electronic side — most notably, Matsushita, Sony, Philips, and Toshiba — have agreed on a common format for DVD that will play but not record video on the TV, a standard for DVD to run software and video on the PC is a more contentious issue. Sony and Philips have aligned with Hewlett-Packard to develop a DVD-ROM to replace the CD-ROM and record and play data on computers. They claim that while the electronics industry standard is adequate for the delivery of movies, it isn't robust enough for interactive use on multimedia computers. The consumer electronic manufacturers still remember the marketing fiasco, and the delay in reaching the potential, when they could not agree on a format for video cassette recorders, and came out with both Beta and VHS. If there is no compromise, the fallout for DVD could be equally damaging. Meanwhile, Compaq has the first PC featuring DVD-ROM technology and Microsoft has released its complete Multimedia reference encyclopedia on one DVD-ROM.

DVD will draw two broad audiences: buyers of home entertainment devices such as CD players and VCRs, and buyers of
PCs. While DVD will probably take off faster among the PC
crowd who tend to be early adapters, the consumer electronic
companies are better marketers, notwithstanding Microsoft, and
are likely to set the standards.

Both the consumer electronics and the computer industries
were looking towards DVD as a way of bridging the narrowing
gap between entertainment and computing and shifting the centre of gravity in home entertainment away from the television. A
standards battle will delay the convergence of the two industries
to create ever more powerful multimedia machines for the
home. A greater opportunity belongs to companies that make the
specially designed chips at the heart of new DVD players: ATI
Technologies Inc., C-Cube Microsystems, Oak Technology Inc.,
and SGS-Thomson Microelectronics Limited.

45...DEG↑365...RKDE↓85...SCEB↑22.34...ITS↓956

GRAPHICS AND MULTIMEDIA SOFTWARE

Company	Ticker Symbol
Microsoft	MSFT
Computer Associates	CA
Adobe Systems	ADBE
Autodesk	ADSK
Visio	VSIO
Pixar	PIXR
Borland	BORL
Macromedia	MACR
MetaCreations	MCRE
Corel	COSFF
Micrografx	MGXI

`45...DEG↑365...RKDE↓85...SCEB↑22.34...ITS↓956`

INTERACTIVE GAME COMPANIES

Company	Ticker Symbol
Microsoft	MSFT
Disney	DIS
CUC International	CU
Electronic Arts	ERTS
Pixar	PIXR
The Learning Company	TLC
Broderbund	BROD
GT Interactive	GTIS
Activision	ATVI
Acclaim Entertainment	AKLM
Spectrum Holobyte	MPRS
T-HQ	THQI
3DO	THDO
7th Level	SEVL

AEROSPACE AND BIOTECHNOLOGY

Five or six years ago, $500 million in investment generated $10 billion in stock market value, a ratio of 20 to 1. Applying the same multiplier today, $2 billion of shareholder equity in the biotech group indicates a $40-billion industry.

Cameron Groome, biotechnology analyst,
First Marathon Securities Limited

Some people don't include aerospace and biotechnology as a part of the technology sector because it doesn't involve computers. However, like the other technology subsets, they are based on intellectual property, and to assess the risk factor is a similar process. Many of the companies in these two industries have large research and development components in their expense mix so they are pushed by new technologies. When you buy computer technology, you are buying applied science. When you buy aerospace and biotechnology, you are buying pure science.

Aerospace

High Tech versus Advanced Tech

There's a difference between high tech and advanced technology. We are not a high-tech business in the way a software company is thought of as high tech. Advanced technology is certainly used in the design and the manufacturing of aircraft and associated products, which in our case includes flight simulators. Our business tends to be more evolutionary rather than revolutionary, and our products don't change so quickly that the market ends up being totally different overnight.

Robert E. Waite,
vice-president of corporate relations and marketing, CAE Inc.

Besides technology, the aerospace industry is driven by a lot of other issues including distribution and political issues. Military applications generate new technology and, especially in the electronics area, the aerospace and aeronautic companies have been responsible for numerous breakthroughs. Because of the nature of their business, they can't quite capitalize on it to get the exciting rates of growth you see in other technology businesses. The aeronautics sector is a cyclical business. Active in air trafiic management and spacecraft, CAE Inc. is best known for its flight simulators, sort of grown-up video games for pilots to practise on. CAE's few customers include Bombardier, Boeing, and Airbus, and their customers in turn are airlines such as Air Canada, American Airlines, and British Airways. Since the airline business is affected by the economy and business cycles, so is CAE.

The software, simulating the performance of an aircraft, is complex and takes a lot of software code writing, creating visual databases to replicate more than 50 airports around the world. At the push of a button, your eyes tell you that you are flying into the airport at Hong Kong, the US Virgin Islands, or Greenland while you're still sitting inside the simulator. A flight simulator costs $15 million dollars so the contracts for CAE are no small order.

Unlike other software manufacturers, CAE won't find itself suddenly outflanked by a brand new technology. "Three people in a garage could not do it," Robert Waite says. "It's too complex and not a simple homespun technology solution. It surprises people to learn that out of 3,700 people at our manufacturing facility in Montreal, there are 1,500 software engineers and that software is a key component."

The aerospace analysts pay as close attention to CAE as the tech analysts do to their sector. "We don't have a lot of trouble attracting investment analysts into our facility to try one of these things," says Robert Waite "There is a general fascination with simulation and the concept of virtual reality. If you invite somebody in to watch a chip being manufactured, it doesn't quite have the same cachet as sitting in the left-hand cockpit seat of a Boeing 777 and flying it."

"It's pretty leading-edge stuff," says Ted Larkin, aerospace analyst for Bunting Warburg. "A lot of it comes from military applications and it's really exciting."

Still, CAE's growth strategy is conservative. There is not a lot of risk for the investor when the backlog of orders stretches for more than two years. And CAE does not want to portray itself as a volatile company that could double in size every year. There have been suggestions that packaging their flight simulator for sale as a video game might create another profit centre. But competing with Sega and Nintendo is not CAE's style. "That's like the movie business, very hit or miss," Mr. Waite says. "We could be doing very well one day and be ousted by somebody else almost overnight. People can be quite fickle when it comes to the latest Nintendo game."

A Brief History of Biotechnology

Biotechnology could not have started before 1953, when James Watson and Francis Crick discovered the molecular structure of DNA. That allowed for the genetic engineering of DNA and the transplanting or splicing of genes from one species into the cells of another. Such DNA becomes part of the host's genetic make-up and is reproduced to change hereditary traits or produce biological products.

Genetic engineering involves techniques used to obtain patents on human genes and to create patentable living organisms. The first to use these newly synthesized molecules for their effect against bacteria were chemical companies, but they didn't have the biological expertise to determine which molecules would work against which diseases. The biotechnology industry really started with the involvement of the pharmaceutical companies, and specifically Connaught Labs, which devised human insulin, the first product recombining DNA to produce a protein.

If you consider the definition of biotechnology to be a method of altering an organism for medical purpose, then the earliest smallpox vaccines developed by Edward Jenner 200 years ago were biotechnology products. Just as Jenner, who laid the foundations of modern immunology as a science, isolated and weakened cowpox bacteria in his lab and administered it to his patients to induce an immune response against smallpox, modern scientists are using genetic engineering to create or change a living organism to meet a medical or social need.

But biotechnology isn't only about human diseases. It's also about agriculture, chemicals, and animal diseases. Genetically engineered products include bacteria designed to efficiently break down oil slicks and industrial waste products, plants that are resistant to diseases and insects or that yield fruits or vegetables with desired qualities, and drugs such as human insulin and interferon.

Hundreds of companies are applying biotechnology techniques to humans, and others are using it for plant and animal hus-
bandry. While relieving human suffering is a noble cause for
research, every kitchen table in the world is the potential market
for genetically enhanced food. Agribusiness giant Monsanto has
spent more than $1 billion on research into agricultural genetics.

Biotechnology stocks are on the roulette wheel of the stock
market casino. The odds of hitting the right number are long, but
the pay-out could be substantial. Amgen is the epic story of hitting the biotechnology jackpot. In 1988, the company had an
intriguing idea — to use genetically engineered bacteria to create
human protein that could be combined into drugs. A $10,000
investment in Amgen in 1988 is now worth $225,000, adjusted for
splits. But the stock market isn't a casino. While it is still a gamble, with research the careful investor can turn the tables and
have the house advantage. Analysts claim they can predict the
probability of success in this sector with a reasonable degree of
accuracy over the long term; however, the precision of the prediction decreases over the short term.

Keeping Up to Date

Today, the entire biotechnology sector is worth $80 billion, less
than the $100-billion value of a single pharmaceutical company,
Merck & Co. Inc. While Merck carries a valuation greater than
the entire sector, aggressive investors look to the biotech companies for the returns that come from novel, innovative products. Robertson Stephens & Company, a primary underwriter of
biotech offerings, estimated that over $5 billion in equity capital
was raised for new issues in the sector in 1996.

Cameron Groome is a young man, but as the biotechnology
analyst for First Marathon Securities Ltd. for six years, he has the
distinction of having done it longer than anyone else in the

Canadian market. "When I started in 1991, there were 13 companies in total, and six that were of any of consequence." The Vec-
tor Securities Biotech Index, which tracks the American
biotechnology market, had 27 stocks. Now there are more than
340 publicly traded biotechnology companies.

In the early years, Groome remembers many of the biotechnology stocks soaring on promises, without accompanying products, revenues, or even good science. The most important
member of the company was the stock promoter, even more than
in the mining and resource sector. Since then, the image of
biotechnology has improved somewhat, but the number of products that have actually achieved commercial success are still few.

The list of superstar biotechnology companies that have made
it is short. Amgen, with revenues for 1996 of $2.2 billion, is no
longer considered by some to be in the class of biotechnology
companies, but has transcended to the realm of pharmaceuticals
as it continues to grow with its biologically engineered blood
products. Biogen, founded in 1978, has had success with products
based on the genetically engineered interferon gene and hepatitis
B antigens. Chiron, the world's second-largest biotechnology
company — with $1.3 billion in revenues from diagnostic, vaccine,
and therapeutic products for many diseases including AIDS,
hepatitis C, and cancer — is 49.9 per cent owned by the giant
Ciba-Geigy Limited of Basel, Switzerland. Eleven of Genentech's
biotechnology-based products are on the market and with its
majority stockholder, Roche Holdings Ltd., of Basel, Switzerland,
it had revenues in 1996 of $968 million, mainly from its growth
hormone product. Genzyme develops and markets pharmaceuticals, genetic diagnostic services, and tissue-repair products for the
treatment of cartilage damage, severe burns, chronic skin ulcers,
and neurodegenerative diseases. About one-third of the biotechnology sector's capitalization is in the handful of these established companies. Meanwhile few of the other 340 biotechnology

public companies have been able to make that breakthrough to get an approved product to market.

Experience Counts

Biotechnology investments have to make economic as well as medical sense. This is not a sector where you can afford to pay people to learn on the job, and the canny investor looks for legitimate science first and then for experienced management. Biotechnology companies are essentially research laboratories testing out new products. Their potential is in developing a blockbuster product and selling it under licence to an established drug company such as Biogen and Chiron, or getting that rare opportunity to become a major pharmaceutical company themselves, like Amgen.

A good thing for investors to watch for is the alliances the new biotechnology companies are making. Even with a Ph.D., it is difficult to independently analyse a company's science. But the large pharmaceuticals have the scientific knowledge and the marketing comprehension to know if the product can be a commercial winner. By the time most biotechnology companies go public, they have at least one major corporate ally with the rights to co-develop and market the products. The size and quality of the deal can tell you how much the pharmaceutical wants the product. The deal should include a guaranteed upfront payment that includes equity of at least $10 million, research and development funding, milestone payments as the research hits benchmarks, and royalties for any sales. Check the details of the agreement carefully because a deal that is contingent on too many milestones being met is less than a deal

Another strategy to limit the sector's bloodcurdling risk is to invest in the established blue chip pharmaceutical giants that are themselves trying to cash in on the biotechnology boom through partnerships, just as Ciba-Geigy and Roche have profited from Genetech and Chiron. "You develop the first drug to a point, then you hand it off to a big brother," Cameron Groome says. "You learn from them, and the next product you take a little bit further along, and gradually you build up your infrastructure and your competency."

In the technology sector generally, and even more in biotechnology, marketing is paramount. In the development stage, the biotechnology company markets to the investment community with a constant barrage of press releases touting their possibilities. Investors have to remind themselves that it can be a long wait between a press release and a product release.

If a company comes up with a new drug that solves a medical problem and it gets approval, the potential is there to turn that intellectual property into a large enterprise. But drugs require manufacturing and distribution, and that's where the pharmaceutical companies come in. In biotechnology, unlike information technology, it is less likely that the company with the invention can go it alone.

"At the beginning, a number of companies set out with the belief that if they have a great idea they can do research and development, clinical and medical testing, and sales and marketing," says Randal Chase, president of Pasteur Merieux Connaught, the large pharmaceutical company that emerged from Connaught Labs. "There are companies that are fabulous research companies but they're terrible at marketing. If they understand their strength, they will work with someone who has that missing component."

The real strength of the major pharmaceutical companies comes from their massive and highly sophisticated sales and marketing networks. Convincing hospitals and physicians a drug is worthwhile is a daunting task. While a young, aggressive biotech company might feel confident with a beefed-up sales force of 50 to 100 representatives, they are pitted against multinational colossi like Merck and Glaxo Wellcome PLC, with their 50,000-plus employees. Merck alone has more employees than the 100 largest biotechnology companies. Even the best drugs won't make it to market against these pharmaceutical juggernauts.

"Good marketing isn't automatic," Randal Chase says. "Enormous sums of money go into the acquisition of expertise. It takes experience and knowledge and resources."

One important component is speed to market. The road to a win comes in assembling the parts of the puzzle quickly. It used to take the pharmaceutical industry 10 to 12 years to develop and launch new products. To take advantage of the impact biotechnology makes, most companies now aim for seven years from conception to fruition.

The other component is globalization. The days are long gone when you could develop a drug for only one market, even an enormous one like the United States. The cost of developing drugs using the newest technologies is expensive and it takes a worldwide effort to be able to pay the bills and generate profit for investors.

Have Patience

Hurry Up and Wait

There's been a disappointment from the investment community at times over how slowly things happen in making major products available. There is an optimism and an expectation that things happen immediately and the longer time lag has been reflected at times in the share prices of particular companies. Our ability is catching up to our earlier expectations. When I look at the literature and at certain clinical trials, I believe biotechnology is going to really take off by the year 2002.

Randal Chase, president, Pasteur Merieux Connaught

Seven years and $200 million is what you are looking at for a biotechnology product to reach the pharmacy shelf. A new drug has to go through several distinct stages of approval and clinical testing before it is approved for sale. If a company seems trapped in a phase of clinical studies for years without moving forward, regard that as a warning sign. When you chart the development of an information-technology company, you can detect a hockey-stick pattern: It goes down and then it shoots up. The chart for biotechnology shows peaks and valleys that match the approval stages. Of course, at each stage along the way, the risk decreases, and sure enough, so do the rewards.

Investors who follow a drug from its preclinical stage through to approval have a chance to make 10, 20, 30, 40, or even 50 times their investment, but the odds of doing it are about 1 per cent. But everybody wants to be there on the day like the one in October 1980 when Genetech opened at $35 and peaked the same day at $88. "You don't pay the same for investing in a company that has a drug in a preclinical stage as you would for investing in a company that has a drug that has been tested on 500 people over five years," biotech analyst Cameron Groome says.

The Biotechnology Pattern

There is an initial excitement when the discovery is announced, but the stock price begins to fall when investors aren't sure the excitement can last. Then there is another period, perhaps the rumblings of a partnership, when the stock trades up again. Then the cycle repeats itself and there is a dip. The final trial data is announced and there is a move up again, then a lull before it gets regulatory approval when it trades higher again. Finally, the worries start about whether the product will go to market. Even a mature biotechnology company can spend millions to research and test a drug, only to see their efforts dissipate in the final stages of development.

The self-confident investor with the time to track the market day to day can try to trade within the peaks. Somebody less venturesome and with less time on their hands should hop on board during a slow period when the excitement has died down and while people are waiting for the next episode in the story to unfold. If you can hit the right point on the continuum and then ride it up, you can score big. But it's a big if.

By their very nature, biotechnology stocks are volatile. No matter what a company tries to do to decrease the downward slope, there is always slippage from the peaks. But if the stock is any good, the slope of the line, with all the troughs, will still beat the market. Biotechnology investors know all about peaks and valleys. From the middle of 1992, they suffered through three years of underperformance until the group took off in the middle of 1995 and gained more than 80 per cent in that year.

The volatility is similar to the resource sector: you discover, you partner, you go through development, and then you go into production. But there are differences: there are no quantum leaps in mining the way there is in biotechnology, and no mineral anywhere near the value human beings place on their own lives.

The Biotechnology Measuring Stick

Once it is established that biotechnology is an area to invest in, there are certain standards to gauge a particular investment. Some are similar to information technology, but the emphasis is different.

1. **Concept.** What is the product? Where is it being developed?

2. **Development stage**. Is it preclinical (a 1 per cent chance of making it), or is it waiting for approval (a 75 per cent chance of making it)?

3. **Efficacy**. Is it significantly more effective than what is available and can it save the health care system money?

4. **Market**. Is there a market for the product? What is it competing against? Has there been a test for market size?

5. **Management**. Is the management team professional or are the scientists still running the show? Nobel laureates are laudable but they don't know anything about product development.

6. **Financials**. Does the company have the wherewithal to carry it forward, or to at least carry it forward to a point where somebody will be willing to be a partner? Remember that it takes $200 million to reach the finish line.

7. **Regulatory**. What stage of approval is it at? Have all the regulatory issues been resolved? Have the studies been designed with the regulators in mind?

8. **Commercial**. How effective is the sales force. Is the marketing partner prepared to help?

9. **Investor sentiment**. Is there an interest in the market place? What is the volume of trade? Has it kept a steady upward slope over the peaks and valleys? Is the company backed by an investment firm that can provide adequate analyst coverage through the good times and the bad?

10. **Promotion**: Has there been a degree of restraint in the promotional claims touting the potential.

One quality the investor is looking for with a biotechnology company is a company that has a stick-to-itive-ness. Too many products in development can indicate an inability to focus. Everybody needs a backup plan, but Cameron Groome says he has heard from too many companies that tell him, "We started working on this but it wasn't really such a big market, so we dropped it and now we are starting to work on that." He tells them, "Finish one thing. Prove that you can take your cell culture system and produce a drug. You don't get drafted to the NHL for almost scoring a goal. You get paid for putting it over the goal line."

Biotechnology and Information Technology

In information technology, products come to market and you can see immediately what the customer acceptance will be. Regulations? What regulations? Biotechnology, even with great technology, has to clear the hurdles of regulation before it gets approved for broad distribution. In the information-technology area, especially software, it's only a matter of time before a product is obsolete or gets leapfrogged by another product. Because they are so easy to reverse-engineer, it is hard to keep a patent on software codes. But with the patent protection in place in Canada for drugs, there is a 17-year lifespan from the time of their creation until a generic manufacturer is allowed to replicate it.

Interestingly, *Forbes* columnist Michael Gianturco has found that when computer stock prices go up biotechnology companies decline. This helps the mutual fund investor. Many funds are called science and technology funds precisely because the investments are in both information technology and biotechnology sectors so that one can counter the other. When prices are high in biotechnology, fund managers buy information technology, and when information technology is high, or fully priced, they use their cash to buy biotechnology.

You can only use one word processor at a time, but there is no limit to the amount of medication someone is prepared to take if they need it. "With new discoveries, new genes, new approaches, and an increase in the amount of knowledge, every day the industry is firing on all cylinders," biotech analyst Cameron

Groome says. What would somebody pay for remission, for their arthritis to go away, to regrow their limbs, or for a new heart? In a wealthy society, the margin on these things is enormous. "When I look at biotechnology companies, I can see how one company with one drug can be a billion-dollar business, and that is going to happen with increasing regularity," says Groome.

Hitting the Home Run

One of the fallacies investors believe about the biotech industry is that every product has to be a billion-dollar blockbuster drug. Moderate $50- or $100-million drugs have made a lot of investors a lot of money. Some companies that have been perceived very favourably have never had a billion-dollar drug. "We did some analysis on home runs versus base hits," Cameron Groome says. "We found a much better probability in making money with base hits than with home runs." Babe Ruth hit 714 home runs but he struck out 1330 times.

The best investments are in companies discovering a treatment rather than a cure. As crass as it seems, an investor is better off with a treatment for cancer that has to be taken day after day than with a single magic cure the patient only has to take once. Equally profitable are drugs that relieve symptoms rather than causes so that they must be taken continuously. The broader the market is for the drug, the more revenue it can achieve. The current best-selling drugs are treatments for anxiety (Prozac and Valium) and ulcers (Tagamet, Pepcid, and Zantac). The ideal drug from an investor's point of view is something relatively expensive with no side effects that you have to take forever. From an investment perspective, you are better off with a treatment for the common cold, not a cure.

"Miraculous cures are few and far between," says Cameron Groome. "There has never been a case of anyone curing a virus with a drug — controlling, yes, suppressing yes, and helping your immune system along, yes — but a pill that you take to make it go away hasn't ever happened."

The other good investment is in a technique rather than a specific product. This makes it harder for a competitor to horn in and replicate the product. It also means the products will keep on coming. For instance, a lot of biotechnology research is currently going on to find better methods of drug delivery. A pill or capsule taken orally is not always the best way to give medicine. Especially with more powerful drugs, research is finding ways of administering drugs through biological membranes by intestinal, nasal, sublingual, transdermal, subcutaneous, intramuscular, intraocular, and other innovative means.

Most biotechnology companies are small-cap start-ups, long on promise, short on cash. They hang on a thread of a single patent or an untested treatment. To hedge the risk, some advisors prescribe taking a small dose and washing it down with a large measure of conventional health care. By investing in the large pharmaceuticals who are allying themselves with the biotechnology enterprises, you aren't counting on one breakthrough; only one in 10 products makes it to the market place. But the large pharmaceuticals have more overhead to carry and one gargantuan success can be offset by other products in the pharmaceutical line reaching maturity.

With so much riding on arcane scientific speculations, biotechnology is one sector where the case for buying a mutual fund, rather than individual stocks, is particularly strong. Even if the investor has done all the homework, it's as hard to isolate the one magic company as it is to find a cure for cancer. If that one company is in the mutual fund bundle, you might not score a four-bagger, but at least you'll get on base.

> I am convinced that there will be some very important new drugs coming out of the biotechnology industry over the next five years. I am not convinced I can zero in on just the two or three companies that will have those drugs. I'd rather own a dozen companies, rather than two or three, and increase my chances of hitting a home run.
>
> *Jim Broadfoot, co-manager,*
> *Mackenzie Universal World Science and Technology Fund*

Mutual fund choices in the biotechnology sector are somewhat limited. There is only one pure open-end biotechnology fund in the US: Fidelity Select Biotechnology. Other conventional health-care funds have significant exposure to biotechnology with most invested in biotech blue chips — in this context, any company with product sales — with the heaviest weightings in Amgen, Biogen, Chiron, and Genentech.

Analysts sometimes rank biotech companies according to their burn rate, the rate at which they are running through their cash. Typically, a biotech company spends more than $200 million buying equipment, paying scientists, and designing experiments in its seven-year odyssey. Since these companies are usually cash rich from stock offerings, but without a product for sale, or revenues, it is possible to calculate the precise date they will run out of money.

Christine Charrette, biotechnology analyst for Nesbitt Burns, says retail investors should understand that biotechnology is a risky sector and not to put their entire portfolio in it. But she says it is a good sector to put a small part of their money in because the growth of these companies can be exceptional. "My attitude towards biotech is buy and hold a long time, and provided that you have good-quality companies, you will do extremely well. There will definitely be ups and downs while the company goes through development. You will have that home run, but it may take a while."

The Future

The demographics in a number of countries are showing an ageing population with specific health needs, and more of these needs than a younger population would have. Since the mid-1980s, about 40 new diseases have been identified, and these are diseases that are most likely going to be treated by drugs created in a laboratory using bioengineering techniques. While nobody wishes for new diseases or populations with health problems, it does mean a profound investment opportunity.

Many firms in the biotechnology sector group are attractive acquisition candidates as firms combine their assets to finance their research and development programs and market their products, or as large pharmaceutical houses pursue strategic alliances with fledgling biotech firms to get access to promising new products.

Meanwhile, regulatory conditions have improved as regulators around the world, including the Food and Drug Administration in the US, speed up the drug approval process and governments allow for less stringent requirements to obtain biotechnology patents. According to the 1996 "Biologics and Biotech Regulatory Report" of product licence applications submitted to the FDA Center for Biologics Evaluation and Research, 60 per cent of submissions got approval in fiscal years 1995 and 1996, up from only 18 per cent in fiscal years 1993 and 1994.

Biotech industry revenues are poised to grow substantially over the next five years. Having commercialized over 30 products in the first 30 years, the biotech industry may have that many successes in the next five years alone. Nearly every disease category — cardiovascular diseases, cancer, inflammatory diseases, immune and infectious diseases, and neurological ailments — is the subject of intense research and development work by the hundreds of biotech firms that now make up the industry. The market being addressed by biotechnology drugs is significant and in many cases entirely unmet by conventional products.

The Marriage of Biotech and Infotech

Microsoft Corporation's Bill Gates is one of the largest biotech investors in the world. He has a personal interest in blending biotechnology with information technology to create yet another new technology segment, which has been named bioinformatics. Bioinformatics is the science of using computing techniques to analyse data obtained by experiments, modelling, and database research, and mining the information useful to the biologist, in particular, the molecular biologist, for new connections and understandings. "Biotechnology and information sciences will be the two dominant scientific and industrial technologies of the twenty-first century," says Bill Gates.

```
45...DEG↑365...RKDE↓85...SCEB↑22.34...ITS↓956
```

BIOTECHNOLOGY COMPANIES WITH SALES OVER $10 MILLION

Company	Ticker Symbol
Genentech	GNE
Chiron	CHIR
Centocor	CNTO
BioChem Pharma	BCHE
Watson Pharmaceuticals	WPI
Immunex	IMNX
Biogen	BGEN
ICN Pharmaceuticals	ICN

```
45...DEG↑365...RKDE↓85...SCEB↑22.34...ITS↓956
```

Genzyme General Division	GENZ
Agouron Pharmaceuticals	AGPH
Sepracor	SEPR
Gilead Sciences	GILD
MedImmune	MEDI
Jones Medical Industries	JMED
Protein Design Labs	PDLI
Vivus	VVUS
Life Technologies	LTEK
Vertex Pharmaceuticals	VRTX
IDEC Pharmaceuticals	IDPH
Bio-Technology General	BTGC
COR Therapeutics	CORR
Ligand Pharmaceuticals	LGND
Interneuron Pharmaceuticals	IPIC
Isis Pharmaceuticals	ISIP
Gensia	GNSA
NeXstar Pharmaceuticals	NXTR
Enzo Biochem	ENZ
Regeneron Pharmaceuticals	REGN
Neurogen	NRGN
Scios	SCIO
Alliance Pharmaceutical	ALLP
Creative BioMolecules	CBMI
Roberts Pharmaceutical	RPC
Cephalon	CEPH
Cell Genesys	CEGE
Amylin Pharmaceuticals	AMLN
U.S. Bioscience	UBS
SEQUUS Pharmaceutical	SEQU
Genzyme Transgenics	GZTC
Liposome Company	LIPO
Oncogene Science	OSIP
Medco Research	MRE
Cytogen	CYTO
NABI	NABI

```
45...DEG↑365...RKDE↓85...SCEB↑22.34...ITS↓956
```

Arris Pharmaceutical	ARRS
Genelabs Technologies	GNLB
NeoRx	NERX
IBAH	IBAH
Synthetech	NZYM
Corvas International	CVAS
Carrington Laboratories	CARN
CellPro	CPRO

BIOTECHNOLOGY COMPANIES WITH SALES UNDER $10 MILLION

Company	Ticker Symbol
North American Vaccine	NVX
PathoGenesis	PGNS
PDT	MRVT
ICOS	ICOS
Sangstat Medical	SANG
Columbia Laboratories	COB
Guilford Pharmaceuticals	GLFD
Neurex	NXCO
QLT PhotoTherapeutics	QLTIF
Zonagen	ZONA
XOMA	XOMA
Pharmacyclics	PCYC
Immune Response	IMNR
Vical	VICL
Molecular Biosystems	MB
Sugen	SUGN
Immunomedics	IMMU
Intercardia	ITRC
Cadus Pharmaceutical	KDUS
Imclone Systems	IMCL
Magainin Pharmaceuticals	MAGN
Northfield Laboratories	NFLD
Aphton	APHT
Unigene Laboratories	UGNE
Somatogen	SMTG

```
45...DEG↑365...RKDE↓85...SCEB↑22.34...ITS↓956
```

VIMRX Pharmaceuticals	VMRX
NPS Pharmaceuticals	NPSP
Medarex	MEDX
BioCryst Pharmaceuticals	BCRX
Alteon	ALTN
Ariad Pharmaceuticals	ARIA
CoCensys	COCN
Shaman Pharmaceuticals	SHMN
Alexion Pharmaceuticals	ALXN
La Jolla Pharmaceutical	LJPC
Cytotherapeutics	CTII
Gliatech	GLIA
Lidak Pharmaceuticals	LDAKA
SciClone Pharmaceuticals	SCLN
Ribi ImmunoChem Research	RIBI
Matrix Pharmaceutical	MATX
Targeted Genetics	TGEN
Onyx Pharmaceuticals	ONXX
Unimed Pharmaceuticals	UMED
Ribozyme Pharmaceuticals	RZYM
Viragen	VRGN
Advanced Magnetics	AVM
GeneMedicine	GMED
Opta Food Ingredients	OPTS
MGI Pharma	MOGN
Anergen	ANRG
Alpha-Beta Technology	ABTI
T Cell Sciences	TCEL
AMBI	AMBI
Cytel	CYTL
ImmuLogic Pharm	IMUL
AutoImmune	AIMM
Cambridge NeuroScience	CNSI
Connective Therapeutics	CNCT
Cortex Pharmaceuticals	CORX
Immunogen	IMGN
Neurobiological Technologies	NTII

CONCLUSION:
OPENING THE VAULT

 You have to think like a guerrilla warrior.

Roger McNamee, partner, Integral Partners.

Now that you know the secrets, you can invest in technology stocks with confidence. Technology is the last frontier of the stock market, and as famed Silicon Valley investor and partner with Integral Partners, Roger McNamee says, to win in this market, you have to develop confidence in your own judgement. There is no shortage of opportunities in this fast-growing sector. Everybody wants to find the next Microsoft, Intel, or Cisco. The next Big One is out there in this sector among the growing number of companies in the semiconductor, hardware, software, telecommunications, networking, Internet, wireless, multimedia, and biotechnology businesses. The challenge is to cut through the hype and understand the true potential.

Pick Me, Pick Me

With so much looking good, here's how you choose the true technology winners:

- The management team has the experience and skills to develop a technology business.

- There are solid finances backing the company.

- The product is truly unique and useful right away.

- There is a clearly defined market and a well-articulated strategy for delivering the product to the market.

- The company's market niche enjoys high profit margins and shows signs of significant growth.

- The company isn't going head-to-head with Microsoft.

- There is a clear opportunity to make a substantial return on investment.

- Timing is everything.

One Last Word about Risk

The high risk in the technology sector is not tied to the overall market risk. Use the risk to your advantage, but just because you are taking a risk doesn't mean you shouldn't be prudent. All prospective investments should be evaluated in terms of the trade-off between risk and reward. The expected return on an investment may be based largely on its historical performance, but, because the technology sector is constantly reinventing itself, there is no guarantee that the future will repeat the past. Investors in this volatile market need a longer time frame and a greater risk tolerance than is necessary for other, less volatile forms of investment. Historical returns on long-term technology investments have been relatively high, but stock prices tend to move rapidly and to greater extremes than with most other investments. Potential technology investors should reflect on how much their financial and emotional comfort could be tested in periods of uncertainty.

The volatility of the sector, while unsettling on a day-to-day basis, is the price you pay to participate in long-term growth. It enables you to sell some stocks at higher prices than would otherwise have been possible, and to buy others at bargain prices. When the news is bad and people are panicking, that's when you should be assessing whether the time is right to pick up a bargain. For investors with a long-term time horizon and a willingness to ride out the volatility, a meaningful portion of their invested capital should be in technology stocks.

As you choose among the various technology options, always determine whether you are investing or speculating. Although the line between the two blurs sometimes, an investment is a thought-out commitment of funds from which you expect to receive a reasonable return and typically involves a longer time horizon than speculation. You are willing to let wealth build gradually rather than looking for a quick bonanza. That doesn't mean you should never speculate; just keep it at an appropriate level for your own comfort and recognize the hazards.

Summing Up the Secrets

1. **Do Your Homework**. Kick the tires as you would when buying a car. Read the newspapers, watch the business shows on television, and follow the hot analysts. They have insider knowledge, but so do you. You know best what appeals to you. Just because I am less keen on the Internet than most of the sector followers doesn't mean it is no good for you. You've seen my reasoning, now use your own. In the end, you have to keep your own counsel, make your own mistakes, and earn your own good fortune.

2. **Spread Your Bets**. Use technology to balance your portfolio, and then diversify within the sector. Technology doesn't

move as a monolith, and buying different segments is a good way to catch the magic.

3. **Check the Quality.** Think fundamentally. Examine the nature of the company's business, the skills of its management, and its market prospects. The company has to be serving a current need in the market place. This is especially true for new and smaller firms. But do not be fooled by the size of the company. Small can be beautiful.

4. **Crunch the Numbers.** While gut instincts are important in this sector, they should always be supported by a calculator. Corroborate your intuition with information by examining the balance sheet and scrutinizing the ledger.

5. **Don't Panic.** Buy good stocks on sale. If you sell into a bear market, you are turning your paper losses into real ones. Selling in a frenzied market means missing out on the earliest, biggest gains as a stock recovers.

6. **Go with What You Know.** The fact of the matter is that Peter Lynch never did like the technology sector, but his philosophy of going with what you know is still valid. Technology has taken over more and more of our lives, and we all have personal experience with it. Cash in on it.

7. **Don't Try to Time the Market.** Technology has a mind of its own, and technology stocks move more because of the innovativeness of its products than because of the direction of the market.

8. **Know When to Sell.** If you have done your homework, you'll recognize if a stock is performing as well as you expect it to. You want to sell because the time is right, not out of sorrow or regret.

9. **Buy a Mutual Fund**. Let a professional think for you. Sure everybody likes to go it alone, but the technology sector can be tricky and, for many investors, a mutual fund is the solution to the puzzle. Having a mutual fund money manager follow the daily ups and downs of this quirky market, saves a lot of aggravation and may just bring the extra edge that will let you score big.

10. **Form an Investment Club**. By getting together with other investors in an investment club you are compounding the brainpower that goes into making investment decisions. There are so many factors to juggle in the technology sector that sharing the load increases the payoff. It is also a good way for investors new to the sector to get their bearings.

Go Forth and Multiply Your Wealth

Now that you know the basics of investing in the technology sector, you can appreciate how exciting the outlook is. The prevailing image, when considering the prospects, is the idea of the home run. Winning in the sector also happens by consistently getting on base, working your way around the diamond and scoring. But the technology game is still young. It's only in its second or third inning, and there are lots of chances to add to the runs. By investing in technology you are investing in the future. The future should be a part of everybody's portfolio.

GLOSSARY

Acquisition The act of one corporation acquiring a controlling interest in another. In an "unfriendly" takeover, the buying corporation may offer incentives to stockholders such as offering a price well above the current market value.

Aggressive Buying Buying shares in small or speculative growth companies to achieve maximum capital appreciation.

Alpha The measurement of the volatility of the market as a whole, rather than a particular stock (See: beta; volatility.)

Analogue The traditional method of transmitting signals where the radio wave is based on electrical impulses. (See: digital.)

Analyst An individual in a brokerage firm or mutual fund group who researches corporations, industry groups, and the market to make buy and sell recommendations on specific securities. A majority of analysts specialize in a particular industry.

Annual Meeting A stockholder meeting that is held yearly. Functions of an annual meeting are for corporate executives to report on the year's results, to elect the board of directors, and to transact other business. The chief executive officer customarily makes a statement on the outlook for the next year and conducts a question-and-answer period.

Annual Report A yearly statement of a corporation's financial condition that describes its operations and provides its balance sheet income statement, and other information that shareholders will be interested in.

Ask The lowest price a broker asks customers to pay for a security. (See: bid.)

Auction Market Exchanges such as the New York Stock Exchange System where brokers competitively bid for the most advantageous price. Unlike conventional auctions with one auctioneer and many buyers, here there are many buyers and sellers. It is distinguished from the over-the-counter market, such as NASDAQ where trades are bought by dealers. (See: over-the-counter.)

Average Down A strategy used to reduce the average price paid for a security by buying additional shares of the security at lower prices.

Bandwidth The amount of data a computer network connection can carry at any given time. The greater the bandwidth, the faster the data transfer capability. When a lot of people are using the same lines to access the Internet, the bandwidth becomes "crowded" and the data flow to your computer slows down. For analogue signals, the width is in the frequency domain, expressed in Hz. For digital signals, the width is in the time domain, expressed in bits per second.

Bear Market Much like a hibernating bear, the market retreats into a deeper slumber and is characterized by a prolonged period of falling stock prices. This is often brought on by a fear of a declining economy. (See: bull market.)

Beta The measure of a particular stock's volatility relative to the stock market as a whole. The higher the beta, the more wildly the stock could swing as the market conditions change. A stock with a lower beta will normally rise and fall more slowly than the market. High betas are for those with strong stomachs; low betas, for those with a low threshold for risk A beta of less than 1 indicates lower risk than the market; a beta of more than 1 indicates higher risk than the market. (See: alpha; volatility.)

Bid The highest price a broker is willing to pay at a given time for trading a unit of a given security. (See: ask.)

Biotechnology The use of biological processes or genetic engineering, as through the exploitation of living organisms or biological systems, in the technological solution to a problem.

Bull Market A charging stock market, or one continuing to rise with a great deal of stock and bond trading. The anticipation of an expanding economy or lower interest rates can set the bulls running. (See: bear market.)

Buy-and-Hold Strategy An investment strategy whereby an investor acquires shares of a corporation to keep over many years.

Buy on the Bad News An investment strategy established from the belief that a security's price will plunge shortly after the corporation reports bad news. Investors who buy at this time deem that the security's price will rise when the news improves.

Byte From the expression "by eights." A unit of storage equal to eight bits that can store a single letter of a word in a document or a dot helping to form a graphic on a computer screen. (See: gigabyte; kilobyte; and megabyte.)

CD-ROM An acronym for Compact Disc–Read Only Memory. A CD-ROM is much like an audio CD only instead of sound, it holds applications or data to be used by the computer. Because it is "read only," you can't record anything on a CD- ROM, but the computer can read whatever is on it.

Call An option giving the holder the right to buy a specific number of shares of an underlying security at a specified price by a fixed date. (See: put.)

Capital Wealth that is available to be used to create even more wealth.

Capitalization The sum of a corporation's value calculated by multiplying the number of shares by the price of each share. (See: large-cap company; mid-cap company; micro-cap company; small-cap company.)

Cash Flow The money received by a business minus the money paid out. The cash receipts or net income from one or more assets for a given period, reckoned after taxes and other disbursements. Often used as a measure of corporate worth.

Chip A small piece of semiconducting material (usually silicon) on which an integrated circuit is embedded. A typical chip is less than $\frac{1}{4}$-square inches and can contain millions of transistors. Computers consist of many chips placed on electronic boards called printed circuit boards. (See: integrated circuit; microprocessor; semiconductor.)

Corporation A legal entity owned by stockholders who have limited liability — that is, they can only lose what they invest. Transfer of ownership is accomplished through the sale of stock shares.

Correction A downward movement in a security's price. Corrections should be expected — no market, or security, moves straight up or down.

Cyclical Stock A stock that is strongly affected by changes in economic activity. The stock's price will rise when the economy turns up, and fall when the economy turns down. Most cyclical industries produce durable goods such as raw materials and heavy equipment. Examples are automobiles and paper stocks. Non-cyclical stocks, such as those within the food and hospital industries, are not directly affected by economic changes. (See: defensive stock.)

Day Order An order to buy or sell securities at a certain price that expires if not executed on the day it is placed.

Dead Cat Bounce Theory Describes a stock's tendency to have a short-term rebound immediately following a significant pull back. These rebounds occur even if the pull back was caused by bad news. The rationale is that no matter how dead a cat is, if you slam it against the ground hard enough, it's bound to bounce a little.

Dealer An individual or firm in the securities business who acts as a principal rather than as an agent in a specific transaction. Dealers buy and sell securities for their own account, and their profit or loss is derived from the difference between the price paid for the security and the price received when selling the security to a customer. Because most individuals and firms act as both brokers and dealers, the term broker-dealer is also used. (See: NASDAQ.)

Defensive Stock Security that is steadier than average. Because of the corporation's business (e.g., utility and food industries), its securities are relatively resistant to general economic changes. Thus, when the stock market is weak, defensive securities are apt to decline less than the overall market. (See: cyclical stock.)

Derivative An investment vehicle that derives its value from the value of another underlying asset. Futures contracts and options are among the most common types of derivatives. (See: futures; options.)

Digital A device or method that uses variations in voltage, frequency, amplitude, and location, to encode, process, or carry binary (zero or one) signals for sound, video, computer, or other information data. Digital communications technology permits higher speeds of transmission with a lower error rate than can be achieved with analogue technology. (See: analogue.)

Dip A small drop in the price of a security after a prolonged up-trend. Analysts frequently advise investors to buy on dips because it is seen as only a temporary price weakness.

Discount Broker A brokerage firm that executes buy-and-sell orders at lower commission rates than those charged by a full-service broker, but without offering any additional services such as research. (See: full-service broker.)

Diversification A risk-management technique that mixes a wide variety of individual stocks within a portfolio, thus minimizing the impact of any one security on overall portfolio performance. When some stocks are not performing well, most likely others are, so you are not in a situation in which you are depending on one particular stock to perform well all the time.

Dollar-Cost-Averaging An investment strategy that involves consistently buying equal dollar amounts of a security at regular intervals regardless of the price, rather than a certain number of shares. As a result, more shares are bought when prices are low than when they are high. Thus, the average cost is less than the average of the prices paid.

Dow Jones Industrial Average A price-weighted daily average of actively traded blue chip stocks. Dating from 1896, it is the oldest and most widely quoted of all the market indicators. It indicates whether prices of stocks in general on the New York Stock Exchange go up or down.

Downside Risk An assessment as to the extent that a security could decline in value considering all possible factors that could affect the security's market price.

Downtick The next trade at a lower price than the previous trade. (See: uptick.)

Dual Listing A security that is listed on more than one exchange — NASDAQ and a regional exchange or the American Stock Exchange and a regional exchange. Being dual listed increases the liquidity of a security (See: liquidity.)

Due Diligence The careful investigation to ensure that all material information pertinent to an issue has been disclosed to prospective investors.

Earnings The amount of profit a corporation receives after expenses and taxes are paid.

Earnings Per Share The amount of a corporation's earnings that is apportioned to each outstanding share. It is calculated by dividing net income by the number of outstanding common shares.

Equity Financing Raising money for working capital or for capital expenditures by selling stock to individual or institutional investors. In return for the money paid, the individuals or institutions receive ownership interests in the corporation.

Financial Statement A record of the financial status of an individual, company, or association. The financial statement includes a balance sheet, an income statement, and may also include other financial analysis such as a cash flow statement.

Full-Service Broker A broker who provides a variety of brokerage and financial services to clients, including offering advice on investment decisions. Generally full-service brokers charge higher commissions than discount brokers who execute trades but do not give any investment advice. (See: discount broker.)

Fully Valued The price at which a corporation's fundamental earnings power is fully reflected in the security's market price. If the stock goes up from that price, it is considered to be overvalued. If the stock goes down, it is undervalued (See: overvalued; undervalued.)

Fundamental Analysis Research and examination of a corporation's financial statements and balance sheets to predict the future price movements of its stock. Among other indicators, fundamental analysts study past records of assets, earnings, sales, products, management, and markets to predict future trends. (See: technical analysis.)

Futures Contracts covering the purchase and sale of financial instruments for future delivery on a commodity futures exchange. (See: derivative; options.)

Gigabyte A unit of storage equal to 1 billion bytes, or in a more strict sense, 1,024 megabytes, used to measure the capacity of hard disks. (See: byte; megabyte.)

Going Long Buying and holding stock.

Going Short (short selling) Borrowing and selling a security that the seller does not own, or any sale that is completed by the delivery of a security borrowed by the seller. Such sales are made in anticipation of a decline in the price of the security to enable the seller to cover the sale with a purchase at a later date at a lower price. Short sellers assume that they will be able to buy the stock at a more favourable price than the one at which they sold short. Securities and Exchange Commission rules allow investors to sell short only when a stock price is moving upward.

Growth Fund A mutual fund that seeks long-term capital appreciation by selecting corporations to invest in that should grow more quickly than the general economy. Growth funds are volatile and they usually rise more quickly in bull markets and fall more sharply in bear markets.

Growth Stock Stock of a company with earnings growing at a fairly rapid rate that is anticipated to continue to grow at high levels. Growth stocks are riskier investments than average stocks. They generally have higher price to earnings ratios and make little or no dividend payments to shareholders.

Hardware The physical components of a computer system, including peripherals such as printers, modems, keyboards and mice. (See: software.)

High-Tech Stock Companies whose business is in high-technology fields such as computers, telecommunications, and biotechnology. High-tech companies have above average earnings growth and volatile stock prices.

Historical Trading Range Price range that a security has traded since going public. Technical analysts perceive the top of a historical range as the resistance level and the bottom as the support level. If a security breaks above the resistance level or below the support level, this is interpreted to mean that the security will reach new highs or lows and its historical trading range expands.

Home Run A big success. Large gains obtained by an investor in a short time period. Aiming to hit a home run is intrinsically more risky than the strategy of holding for the long term.

Hub A group of circuits connected at one point on a network enabling traffic concentration and economies of scale.

Index Statistical measurement of groups of securities, industries, or markets that reflect market prices for the companies in the index. Stock indexes are used as a base for trading index options.

Institutional Investor An organization, such as an insurance company, mutual fund, or pension fund, that trades securities in large enough share quantities or dollar amounts that it qualifies for preferential treatment and lower commissions. Institutional investors are covered by fewer protective regulations than individual investors because it is assumed that they are more knowledgeable and better able to protect themselves. (See: retail investor.)

Internet A diverse and global collection of networks and computers all linked together.

Integrated Circuit An electronic circuit in which many active or passive elements such as transistors, resistors, capacitors, and diodes are fabricated and connected together. (See: chip; microprocessor; semiconductor.)

Internet Service Provider (ISP) A company or organization that provides connections to the Internet.

Intranet An internal and private network inside a company or organization that works much like the Internet.

Investment Bank An institution in the business of raising capital for corporations.

Investment Club Individuals who pool their funds to make joint investments with purchases determined by a vote of the members. The clubs permit investors with small dollar amounts to participate in larger investments and pay lower commissions. It also assists club members in becoming more knowledgeable about investing. There are over 30,000 investment clubs in North America.

Investor Relations Department A department within a publicly-listed corporation that is responsible for investor relations. The department's functions include: assuring that a company's activities and objectives are understood by the investment community; ensuring full and timely disclosure of material information, and responding to requests from shareholders, institutional investors, and brokers for information and written material such as its quarterly and annual reports.

IPO An initial public offering is the first public issuance of stock from a company that has not been publicly traded before.

January Effect The period when stock prices have historically tended to rise considerably. The January Effect is caused by year-end selling for tax losses, recognizing capital gains, or portfolio window dressing. Even though the sell-off depresses the stocks, it has nothing to do with their basic worth and bargain hunters tend to buy in and cause the January rally.

Java A network-oriented computer programming language invented by Sun Microsystems for programs that are safe and easy to download through the Internet. Using Java, Web pages can feature things like animation, calculations, and games.

Kilobyte A unit of storage equal to 1024 bytes or 8192 bits. (See: bit; byte; kilobyte; megabyte.)

Large-Cap Company A company with a total market value of $5 billion or more. (See: capitalization; mid-cap company; micro-cap company; small-cap company.)

Liquidity The ease with which an investment can be convert-
ed to cash in the market place. A large number of buyers
and sellers and a high volume of trading activity provide
high liquidity.

Macroeconomics Analysis of the overall economy using information such as unemployment, inflation, production, and
price levels.(See: microeconomics.)

Market Makers The securities dealers, specifically the NAS-
DAQ member firms, that use their own capital, research,
and resources to represent over-the-counter stock by
standing ready to buy or sell the stocks they represent.
Each Market Maker competes for customer order flow by
displaying buy-and-sell quotations for a guaranteed number
of shares. Once an order is received, the Market Maker will
immediately purchase for, or sell from, its own inventory
and seek the other side of the trade until it is executed,
often in a matter of seconds. The NASDAQ Stock Market is
a decentralized network of competitive Market Makers.
(See: NASDAQ.)

Market Maker Spread The difference between the price at
which a Market Maker is willing to buy a security and the
price at which the firm is willing to sell it (i.e., the difference between a Market Maker's bid and ask for a given
security.) Since each Market Maker positions itself to either
buy or sell inventory at any given time, each individual
Market Maker spread is not indicative of the market as a
whole.

Market Timing Determination of when to buy or sell securities through use of fundamental or technical indicators.

Megabyte A unit of storage equal to 1024 kilobytes, 1,048,576
bytes, or 8,388,608 bits. (See: bit; byte; kilobyte;
megabyte.)

Microeconomics Analysis of the behaviour of economic units such as companies; industries; or households. (See: macro-economics.)

Microprocessor A silicon chip that contains a central processing unit (CPU). The "brains" behind all personal computers, microprocessors also control the logic of almost all digital devices, from clock radios to fuel-injection systems for automobiles. (See: chip; integrated circuit; semiconductor.)

Micro-Cap Company A company with a market value of $100 million or less. (See: capitalization; large-cap company; mid-cap company; small-company.)

Mid-Cap Company A company with a market value of between $1 billion and $3 billion. (See: capitalization; large-cap company; micro-cap company; small-cap company.)

MMX A designation for a particular model of the Intel Pentium microprocessor line. The Pentium MMX chip is designed to boost the performance of many audio, video, and image-processing applications. Games and many multimedia software titles perform better on computers equipped with the MMX chip, especially software applications written specifically to take advantage of it.

Multimedia The use of more than one medium; such as any combination of sound, graphics, animation, and video. A multimedia computer typically has speakers for sound and a fast microprocessor that can handle graphics, animation, and video, and a multimedia software application that usually contains images, audio, text, video, and animation.

Mutual Fund A fund actively operated by an investment company that raises money from shareholders and invests it on their behalf. A mutual fund offers the investor the benefits of professional management and greater safety and reduced volatility through portfolio diversification. How the fund invests is determined by its objectives.

NASDAQ (National Association of Securities Dealers Automated Quotation System) The NASDAQ Stock Market is an electronic screen-based market comprising about 4000 stock issues with multiple Market Makers negotiating the buying and selling of each stock. This is where most high-tech stocks are traded. (See: Market Makers.)

Network A group of computers and related devices, such as printers, that are connected by cable or some other means so they can communicate with each other.

Odd Lot Any number of shares traded that is less than its normal trading unit (round lot). Typically, an odd lot is 1 to 99 shares with a round lot being multiples of 100 shares.

On-line Connected and ready to communicate with another computer, on-line service, or the Internet. Users are considered on-line when they are connected to a computer service through a modem, that is, they are actually on the line.

Option The right to buy or sell round lots of stock at a specified price before a specified deadline. If the deadline passes without the exercise of that right, the option expires and the option buyer forfeits a premium paid for the option. A call option is the right to buy, while the right to sell is called a put option. (See: call; derivative; put.)

Over-the-Counter (OTC) Market A market for securities that are not listed on an exchange. Security orders are transacted via telephone and a computer network that connects dealers. As opposed to the NYSE, which is an auction market, the OTC is a negotiated market and OTC dealers may act as either principals or agents for customers. NASDAQ is an Over-the-Counter market.

Out-Of-Favour A stock or industry that investors do not currently like. Investors who buy stocks that are out of favour are called "contrarian investors." Their goal is to purchase the stock cheaply and to sell it when their earnings increase.

Overvalued The price of a security which is not justified by its price to earnings ratio and should eventually decline. (See: fully valued; undervalued.)

Pacific Stock Exchange Regional exchange in San Francisco and Los Angeles where a lot of technology stocks are cross-listed.

P/E (Price to Earnings) Ratio The relationship between a stock's price and its earnings per share is calculated by dividing the stock's price per share by earnings per share for a 12-month period. The ratio, also known as the "multiple," gives an investor an approximation of how much they are paying for a corporation's earning power and is a tool for comparing the prices of different common stocks. Low P/E stocks are usually in mature industries with limited growth potential. Companies with high P/E ratios (over 20) are usually up-and-comers that are fast growing but riskier investments.

PCS (Personal Communications System) A ubiquitous digital wireless telecommunications service that will allow "anytime, anywhere" voice and data communication.

Portfolio Manager The person responsible for investing a mutual fund's assets, implementing its investment strategy, and managing day-to-day portfolio trading (also fund manager).

Prospectus The document required to be furnished to all buyers and potential buyers of newly registered securities, which provides detailed information about the company issuing the securities and about that particular offering.

Put A contract that gives the holder the right to sell a specified number of shares of a particular stock, at a predetermined price — called the "strike price" — on or before the option's expiration date. For this right; the holder (buyer) pays the writer (seller) a premium. The holder profits from the contract if the stock's price drops. The writer profits when the underlying security's price remains the same, rises, or drops by less than the premium received. (See: call; option.)

Qualitative Analysis Analysis that looks at a corporation's management experience, employee morale, and the status of labour relations instead of the corporation's financial data.

Quantitative Analysis Analysis that looks at a corporation's financial data and projections.

Research Department A department within a brokerage firm that analyses securities and markets using both fundamental analysis and technical analysis. The analyst makes trading recommendations for the firm's institutional and retail clients (provided by their broker). If followed by many investors, an analyst's recommendations can have an impact on security prices.

Red Herring A preliminary prospectus given to investors when brokers obtain indications of interest. Although the document does not have all the information included in the offering circular, it does include the major facts. A preliminary prospectus is often called a "red herring" because its front-page notice, printed in red ink, states that the preliminary prospectus is "subject to completion or amendment" and "shall not constitute an offer to sell...."

Retail Investor An investor who buys and sells securities on his or her own behalf — not for an organization. Retail investors typically trade in much smaller quantities than institutional investors (also individual investor). (See: institutional investor.)

Return The change in the value or realized profit of investments over an given period stated as an annual percentage rate.

Risk The measurable possibility of losing money because a security's value will substantially decline. Risk is calculated by measuring beta, market variability, earnings variability, growth orientation, immaturity and smallness, low valuation, and financial risk.

Risk/Return Ratio The greater the investment risk — the greater the expected return. One measure of risk and return is the range of possible outcomes. Another measure of risk is price volatility. The ratio places an investor's desire for capital preservation at one end of the scale and a desire to maximize returns at the other end.

Risk Averse An investor who, given different risk alternatives, will choose the security with the least amount of risk.

Russell 2000 Index The principal index for small-cap stocks, measuring the performance of the 2000 smallest companies. The average market capitalization is approximately $467.3 million and the largest company in the index has an approximate market capitalization of $1.1 billion.

Semiconductor A material that is neither a good conductor of electricity (like copper) nor a good insulator (like rubber). The most common semiconductor materials are silicon and germanium. Computer chips are composed of semiconductor materials. Semiconductors make it possible to miniaturize electronic components making them faster and requiring less energy. (See: chip; microprocessor.)

Size of the Market The number of shares in an order a Market Maker is prepared to fill at a particular price.

Small-Cap Company A company with a market value of between $100 million and $1 billion. (See: capitalization;

large-cap company; micro-cap company; mid-cap company.)

Software The instructions that enable a computer to perform functions. The two primary categories of software are systems software, such as operating systems; and applications software that does real work for users, such as word processing, graphics programs, and spreadsheets. (See: hardware.)

Speculator An investor who is willing to assume large risk in return for potentially great rewards by purchasing high-risk investments which may provide above average gains, but also carry a higher than average possibility for loss of principal. A speculator usually buys for the short term.

Specialized Fund A mutual fund whose investment objective is to capitalize on the return potential provided by investing primarily in a particular industry or sector of the economy, such as a technology fund (also sector fund).

Split Increasing the number of outstanding shares in a corporation by dividing the existing shares without affecting shareholders' equity or the total market value at the time of the split. With a two-for-one split, an individual stockholder would end up with twice as many shares, but each would initially be worth only half as much of the original.

Standard & Poor's 500 Index Commonly known as the S&P 500, it is a daily measure of the movement of the stock market based on the averages of 500 widely held common stocks listed on the NYSE chosen by Standard & Poor's Corporation to reflect the industrial balance of the market.

Stock An ownership interest in a company, also known as shares in a company. Stock is issued to raise capital.

Stop-Loss Order An order to a broker to sell at a specified price, the stop price to limit the extent of possible losses.

Technical Analysis Research and examination of the market and securities using charts and computer programs to identify and project price trends. The analysis includes studying price movements and trading volumes of the market as a whole. In contrast to fundamental analysis, technical analysis does not consider a corporation's financial data. (See: fundamental analysis.)

Ticker Symbol A unique all letter code given to all securities trading on the stock market. The symbols identify the corporation and facilitates trading and ticker reporting. Stocks on the New York Stock Exchange are generally identified by three letters and on NASDAQ, by four letters. If a fifth letter appears, it usually identifies the issue as other than a single issue of stock or a stock that also trades on a non-US exchange.

Trader An investor, also known as a day trader, who buys and sells securities to take advantage of price changes within a short time period — sometimes days or hours.

Triple Witching The last trading hour on the third Friday of March, June, September, and December on which stock options, stock index options, and stock index futures all expire simultaneously. There tends to be a large amount of trading as traders and investors attempt to close their positions in the option or underlying stock. This creates a volatile market.

Undervalued A security selling beneath its liquidation value or when analysts believe its price is below what it merits. Fundamental analysts try to identify undervalued corporate stocks to invest in before they become fully valued. Undervalued companies are often takeover targets because acquiring companies can buy the assets inexpensively. (See: fully valued; overvalued.)

Underwriter Investment bankers who handle the offering of a new issue of securities. They buy all the securities from the issuer and distribute them to investors making their profit on the underwriting spread — the difference between the price they pay and the price they charge.

Uptick A transaction executed at a price higher than the preceding transaction in the same security. (See: downtick.)

Venture Capital A source of financing for start-up companies and new ventures that involves investment risk but offers the prospect far above-average future profits. Venture capitalists are commonly rewarded with profits, royalties, preferred stock, and capital appreciation of shares when the company goes public.

Video Conference A discussion between two or more people, each in a different location, but capable of seeing and hearing each other through live video and sound being carried by the telecommunications network.

Volatility The size and frequency of fluctuations in the price of a particular security, sector, or market. A security may be volatile because the company's outlook is uncertain or because the market is. Market-related volatility is measured by alpha. When the reasons for the variation has to do with the particular security, and not the market as a whole, volatility is measured by beta. (See: alpha; beta.)

Volatility Index A measurement of the amount a stock fluctuates in its 52-week high/low price range. Usually expressed as a variance or standard deviation.

World Wide Web (WWW) A popular part of the Internet where information is organized in hypertext which allows the user to click on a link word or title and have a document relating to that word or title instantly appear on the screen.

INDEX